I absolutely loved *The Truth Comes Out*. Once I started reading, I couldn't put the book down. I love how real and authentic Nancy is in sharing her life. I love how she lets us know of her great pain, confusion and spiritual struggles. Her book shows how God has transformed her heart and is a testimony of how God leads and guides us through all of our struggles and pain. Her story offers much hope.

Jan Dravecky
AUTHOR, *A JOY I'D NEVER KNOWN*
WOMEN'S MINISTRY DIRECTOR
WOODMAN VALLEY CHAPEL, COLORADO

Nancy has been to hell and back—not once, not twice, but many times— as she has had to deal with the loss of children and the issue of homosexuality up close and personal. She has learned the depth of God's grace, the power of forgiveness and the peace found in the shelter under God's wings. In this book you will find great wisdom laced with practicality that leads you to a larger understanding and a compassion that brings healing.

Ruth Graham
CHAIRMAN AND FOUNDER, RUTH GRAHAM AND FRIENDS
AUTHOR, *IN EVERY PEW SITS A BROKEN HEART*

Nancy brings a compassion and insight to *The Truth Comes Out* that can only come from personal experience and pain. Not only has she lived through, but she has learned from two of the most traumatic situations any of us could face—learning of her husband's secret homosexual life and losing him to AIDS, then having to face the media firestorm of her daughter's very public declaration of being a lesbian. Her story of God's grace and provision as she navigated her way through these events—seeking to reflect His love and submit to His authority all the while—will be an inspiration to anyone who is unsure how to respond to a loved one's "coming out."

Mike Haley
DIRECTOR OF GENDER ISSUES, FOCUS ON THE FAMILY
CHAIRMAN OF THE BOARD, EXODUS INTERNATIONAL

I have befriended, supported and counseled men and women in conflict with homosexual feelings and behaviors for more than 18 years. I am continuously humbled by their willingness to ask hard questions and explore and challenge some of the most shameful, disappointing and confusing areas of their lives. Many of their parents, spouses, pastors and friends often have no idea what a difficult journey they have personally chosen as they seek to obey God in the realm of relationship and sexuality. That is why I'm so deeply moved and grateful for Nancy's book *The Truth Comes Out*. She did not merely seek to understand another's journey and pain; she entered her *own* journey of self-discovery, growth and healing. In this painstakingly honest book about a *real* family with *real* problems, Nancy highlights the truth that there is no greater gift that we can give to a loved one than to be willing to submit to our own process of redemption. For it is indeed out of the love with which we are loved that we can love another well.

Janelle M. Hallman, MA, LPC
PRIVATE PRACTITIONER AND ADJUNCT FACULTY
DENVER SEMINARY

After walking with Nancy Heche, my dear friend, for oh so many years, through many fires and tests, I can think of no one better to tell you how to find beauty in the ashes of life. Truly this teacher has been a student first. I have witnessed the grace with which she has endured unspeakable trials and rebounded countless times. Not only is she a gifted counselor, but she is also an incredible woman who is a worthy testament to the faithfulness of a God who fashions us into vessels of honor, sometimes through excruciating circumstances that raise unanswerable questions but accomplish incredible results in our character.

Michelle McKinney Hammond
AUTHOR, *THE DIVA PRINCIPLE* AND *UNVEILING THE DIVA MYSTIQUE*

I read *The Truth Comes Out*—every page of it—because I wanted to know what God taught Nancy as she walked through the pain of a marriage broken by homosexuality and the anguish of children variously affected by the sins of their father. Nancy offers no easy answers except that God's grace is sufficient.

Dr. Erwin Lutzer
SENIOR PASTOR, MOODY CHURCH
CHICAGO, ILLINOIS

Nancy Heche knows more than anyone the pain of love and loss, joy alternating with almost unendurable sorrow. Anyone who has a family member living homosexually will understand another challenge Nancy has faced: How to show unconditional love when she disapproved of her loved ones' lifestyles. "Change my hard heart, Lord," Nancy asks—and so began a process that has taken her on a remarkable journey of faithful endurance.

Joseph Nicolosi, Ph.D.
PSYCHOLOGIST AND AUTHOR

Nancy Heche has addressed a most painful and important subject with great depth and tenderness. Any father or mother who struggles to reach out to a child whose path in life is prodigal in any way—using the word as it was originally meant—will find both wisdom, comfort and (the former not necessarily leading instantly to the latter) a way to patience in this heartfelt, insightful chronicle of alienation and love.

Jeffrey Satinover, MD
DEPARTMENT OF PHYSICS
UNIVERSITY OF NICE, FRANCE

Many will read Nancy's incredible life story and say, "How tragic!"
I read it and say, "How faithful!" This is all about God's faithfulness to a
broken lady and her faithfulness, by God's grace, and in the midst of
unthinkable suffering, to Him. Few people have affected my life as profoundly
as Nancy Heche. Read this remarkable book and learn much from a
remarkable woman and an even more remarkable God.

Dr. Sam Storms
ENJOYING GOD MINISTRIES
KANSAS CITY, MISSOURI

The Truth Comes Out is a riveting and inspiring account of one woman's
journey with homosexuality in her family. A modern-day Job, Nancy's life has
been transformed from grief and despair to triumph and redemption through
Jesus Christ. You will be blessed and encouraged by this incredible story.

Carol L. Wagstaff, M.A.
EXECUTIVE DIRECTOR, LIVING STONES MINISTRIES
GLENDORA, CALIFORNIA

Without sugar-coating or seeking sympathy, Nancy weaves her heartbreaking
story in *The Truth Comes Out* in a way that will bring hope and understanding to
many readers. Having known Nancy for more than 20 years, I have seen her
racked with pain beyond endurance and have witnessed the transformation that
God has accomplished in her through forgiveness and acceptance. She doesn't
offer trite answers, but she confidently asserts that God's grace is enough—come
what may. You will be both enlightened and encouraged by her faith journey.

Mary Whelchel
FOUNDER AND SPEAKER
THE CHRISTIAN WORKING WOMAN RADIO MINISTRY

NANCY HECHE

the truth comes out

Regal

From Gospel Light
Ventura, California, U.S.A.

PUBLISHED BY REGAL BOOKS
FROM GOSPEL LIGHT
VENTURA, CALIFORNIA, U.S.A.
PRINTED IN THE U.S.A.

Regal Books is a ministry of Gospel Light, a Christian publisher dedicated to serving the local church.
We believe God's vision for Gospel Light is to provide church leaders with biblical, user-friendly mate-
rials that will help them evangelize, disciple and minister to children, youth and families.

It is our prayer that this Regal book will help you discover biblical truth for your own life and help
you meet the needs of others. May God richly bless you.

For a free catalog of resources from Regal Books/Gospel Light, please call your Christian supplier or contact us at
1-800-4-GOSPEL *or* www.regalbooks.com.

All Scripture quotations, unless otherwise indicated, are taken from the *New International Version*®.
Copyright © 1973, 1978, 1984 by International Bible Society. Used by permission of Zondervan
Publishing House. All rights reserved.

Other versions used are
NASB—Scripture taken from the NEW AMERICAN STANDARD BIBLE®, Copyright © 1960, 1962,
1963, 1968, 1971, 1972, 1973, 1975, 1977, 1995 by The Lockman Foundation. Used by permission.
Phillips—The New Testament in Modern English, Revised Edition, J. B. Phillips, Translator. © J. B. Phillips
1958, 1960, 1972. Used by permission of Macmillan Publishing Co., Inc., 866 Third Avenue, New
York, NY 10022.

© 2006 Nancy Heche
All rights reserved.

Library of Congress Cataloging-in-Publication Data
Heche, Nancy.
  The truth comes out / Nancy Heche.
    p. cm.
  ISBN 0-8307-3912-2 (hard cover)
  1. Heche, Nancy. 2. Ex-gay movement. 3. Homosexuality—Religious aspects—Christianity. I. Title.

BR115.H6H43 2006
261.8'35766—dc22   2006016591

Rights for publishing this book in other languages are contracted by Gospel Light Worldwide, the
international nonprofit ministry of Gospel Light. Gospel Light Worldwide also provides publishing
and technical assistance to international publishers dedicated to producing Sunday School and
Vacation Bible School curricula and books in the languages of the world. For additional information,
visit www.gospellightworldwide.org; write to Gospel Light Worldwide, P.O. Box 3875, Ventura, CA
93006; or send an e-mail to info@gospellightworldwide.org.

"We are meant to speak the truth in love, and to grow up in every way."

—EPHESIANS 4:15, *PHILLIPS*

Family

RICHARD CARELTON PRICKETT (1908–1978)

MARIETTA SUSAN TUKEY PRICKETT (1912–2000)

NANCY ABIGAIL BAKER PRICKETT (B. 1937)

PENELOPE ANN PRICKETT (B. 1937)

HOBART "JOE" HECHE (?–1967)

CLARA BAUMGARTNER HECHE (1898–1986)

DONALD JOE HECHE (1937–1983)

SUSAN CLAIRE HECHE (1957–2006)

CYNTHIA ANNE HECHE (AUGUST 1961–OCTOBER 1961)

NATHAN BRADLEE HECHE (1965–1983)

ABIGAIL ANNE-MARIA HECHE (B. 1966)

ANNE CELESTE HECHE (B. 1969)

Timeline

June 10, 1956: Don and Nancy marry.

May 5, 1957: birth of Susan Claire Heche.

June 1959: Nancy graduates from Indiana University, and the family moves to Cleveland, Ohio. "Born again," baptized and become members in fundamental church.

August 26, 1961–October 26, 1961: Cynthia Anne Heche is born and dies within two months.

1962: Baptism and membership in "true" church.

April 21, 1965: birth of Nathan Bradlee Heche.

August 7, 1966: birth of Abigail Anne-Maria Heche.

May 25, 1969: birth of Anne Celeste Heche.

1972: left "true" church.

1977: moved to east coast.

1983: moved to Chicago.

March 1983: Don dies from AIDS complications.

June 1983: Nathan dies in a car crash.

1988: renewed commitment to Christ.

2003: doctorate in pastoral counseling.

2005: joined Love Won Out conference team; joined Ruth Graham and Friends conference team.

January 2006: daughter Susan dies from cancer.

September 2006 – *The Truth Comes Out* published.

*   *   *   *

Contents

Foreword

Perhaps one of the most challenging issues facing the evangelical Church and our culture is the issue of homosexuality. It's a hot topic in which reason is often obliterated by emotion. The Church has not wanted to deal with it, hoping it will go away. It won't go away. The homosexual community pushes its agenda, which alarms the Church and threatens to split historic denominations. The Church, on the other hand, seems to have forgotten *its* calling and agenda.

Although we preach grace, we have a difficult time extending it when it comes to the homosexual, who may be our coworker, our neighbor, our friend, child, brother, sister, spouse or fellow church member. How are we to respond to them? We don't want to compromise our convictions—we like to keep our theology neat. But is there a balance? Does it have to be either all black or all white?

My friend Nancy Heche has lived with this issue for many years. She has journeyed through the abyss of anger, bitterness and rebellion into a depth and range of emotions. Her book is brutally honest. She courageously tells her own story of dealing with members of her family. She tackles the issues head-on, because she has lived it.

She also lets us into her heart and mind as she wrestles with what clearly was anathema to her and brought her untold heartache. She tried to run away, but God wouldn't let her go far. He brought her to a large place called grace. And as He held up the mirror, the truth came out, and she realized that it was really all about her.

Nancy's story is a clarion voice within the evangelical Christian community—speaking truth and forging a clear path to help us know how to respond to the issues of homosexuality and to the homosexual person.

Don't just stand there! Buy this book. Read this book. I highly recommend it.

Ruth Graham
Author *In Every Pew Sits a Broken Heart*

A Thank-You Note

It took a village to get this book into your hands.

To Mark Sweeney, my persistent and patient agent, who believed my story should be told; Kim Bangs and the Regal team who enthusiastically agreed; Deena Davis, my empathic editor, who held my hand and saw my tears throughout the story-telling; Marcus Brotherton, who organized more than 50 years of story into this one story. Thank you.

To some of the hundreds of people who, after hearing my story, shared their own with me and let me put their stories into this book. Thank you.

To my friends who read my story and endorsed it with encouraging and generous words. Thank you.

To my family and friends who have listened and loved and lived to see the completion of this book. Thank you.

To God. Into Your Hands I commend this story. Thank *You*.

Introduction

When my husband died from AIDS in 1983, I didn't know where to turn for help. I didn't even know if there was anyone who *could* help me. But I didn't want to talk about it anyway. I followed his pattern and chose to keep his secret. Then, 14 years later, when my youngest daughter told me she had fallen in love with a woman, she wouldn't keep it a secret. Everyone knew about it this time. Her parade in the press was a far cry from my husband's earlier cover-up. Still, I didn't know where to turn for help.

One evening, I was driving through the gloomy darkness of Chicago's Kennedy Expressway, thinking about how I've learned the hard way, without much help and with a lot of mistakes. Suddenly I heard a voice from the car radio: "The Love Won Out conference, sponsored by Focus on the Family, provides support for families and loved ones who are dealing with the issue of homosexuality."

What? Come again? I could hardly believe my ears. Help is on the way! Had it been here all along and I didn't know it? Sign me up.

I heard Dr. James Dobson introduce a woman who had lived homosexually for several years and who is now a staff member at Focus. Her current ministry involves helping people understand some of their concerns around their loved one's homosexuality.

"Please listen to her story of healing and ministry," Dr. Dobson said.

Gladly! I hung on to every word of her soft Southern drawl as tightly as I held on to the steering wheel of my speeding car.

She began: "There was a couple in a little church in Kentucky who just loved on me. . . . Later, I met some people from Exodus International, a support group for families and those struggling with homosexuality." Melissa melted my heart with her beautiful story. And she opened the door to the help I needed.

"You mean someone has figured out that we parents and spouses need advice and information and support?" I said, talking out loud to my radio. I turned up the volume to hear every heartening word. This radio broadcast on WMBI, a Christian station in Chicago, was a dream come true, an answer to an old, sad, hopeless prayer.

If there is some help to be given, I wanted to receive it. Maybe I could even give it—maybe I could at least share my experience. For years I had felt so desperate and alone. If I could give an ounce of encouragement to a spouse or another parent who was feeling alone and confused, I was willing.

What would I share if I had the opportunity? All I can really say is that I'm a survivor. I am still standing, fully clothed and in my right mind. I am blessed. My hard heart is being changed and healed. Maybe I could comfort someone with the same comfort I have received. And surely I would get some of the information and resources that I had needed for so long.

There wasn't anyone at my church to whom I could talk. It seemed as if no one else was interested in sexual brokenness, especially homosexuality. The only sex topic we talked about was premarital sex, and maybe abortion once a year. I felt like an outcast.

As a student, I begged for some dialogue around same-sex issues in my counseling classes at Loyola and Northwestern: "Can't anyone help me figure this out? A father and then a daughter? What are the causes of homosexuality?" "What kind of help will we, as counselors in the near future, offer to families who are shocked and confused or hurt or angry about it?" It was a serious challenge: "If we won't be able to help people, who will? Where will they go? Surely we will have clients who ask some of my same questions. Homosexuality is not going away, and we need to have some answers."

"We don't have any real answers for you," was the typical reply. The issue seemed too difficult for everyone. No wonder I cried with relief in the car when I heard the radio program that night.

When I arrived home that evening, I sent an e-mail to Focus on the Family, introducing myself and offering my willingness to serve with them if they had a need for a parent's or spouse's voice or perspective.

In the past, I had adamantly told the Lord, "I'll go anywhere, but just don't ever ask me to do anything around the issue of homosexuality. I'll do *anything* but that. But you know what God does—He always gives us a second chance to get it right—"so that I might show My Power in you and that My Name might be proclaimed in all the earth" (Rom. 9:17).

"Nancy, this is Mike Haley from Focus on the Family. We got your e-mail this week. We've been looking for a parent to share her story at our conferences—a lot of parents show up and ask to hear a parent's story.

Would you be interested in working with us?" It hadn't even been a week since I'd shot off the e-mail.

Hmmmm. When I hear Mike's invitation, one of my favorite Bible verses springs into my head. It's the verse where her Uncle Mordecai says to Queen Esther, "Who knows but that you have come to [the kingdom] for such a time as this?" (Esther 4:14) I have the verse on the scrolling marquee screen saver on my laptop, so it's a daily reminder to me: Who knows, Nancy, but that *you* have come to the Kingdom for such a time as this?

I don't mean to be presumptuous, but I've thought about this verse hundreds of times and how it might apply to me. I have repeated it to my clients, to my students, to my children and grandchildren. I hear it as a challenge, as an invitation, as an opportunity. What's *your* kingdom, Nancy? Is it *your* time?

When my daughter Susan died of brain cancer in January 2006, Abigail, my next oldest daughter, helped take over the responsibilities of home-keeping for the children still living at home—Natalie, 16, and Ben, 13. *Who knows but that she has come to the Kingdom for such a time as this!* It's no accident, I am sure of it.

My client K., who is adopted, and a beautiful Christian woman, wants to connect with her birth family that is not Christian. *Who knows but that K. has come to the Kingdom for such a time as this?* Surely you don't think it's a coincidence.

My amazing students at Judson College and Loyola University are working adults who are hoping to complete their bachelor's degrees. They come from different vocations, cultures and lifestyles, and are thrown together with me as their instructor to encourage and support and facilitate their work. There is a synergy and respect that enables us to grow together. *Who knows but that we have come to this kingdom for such a time as this!*

My students often say, "It's very clear that we're supposed to be together in *this* class. I couldn't fit it into my schedule last semester, but I know I'm supposed to be here now." I know it too. This classroom, this university, this introductory course to adult college life, these special people—this is our kingdom for a few weeks together. *We have come to these kingdoms for such a time as this.* I live my life by this truth.

So when Mike Haley posed his question: "Would you be interested in working with us on an ongoing basis?" I was pretty sure that I had come to the kingdoms of homosexuality and Love Won Out for such a time as this. It has taken almost 25 years for me to be ready, but I trust this is definitely the right thing for me to do.

"Wow, thank you. Tell me what you have in mind," I said.

I snapped out of my reverie about how God has been equipping and preparing me for such a time and got ready to jump in with both feet to work with Mike and Melissa and many other fantastic people in the Love Won Out conferences.

Honestly, I had no idea at the time how much more change was in store for me. Not only would I have the opportunity to learn from many other professionals, but I would also have the opportunity to support and encourage friends and families and congregations and pastors in their journey around the issues of homosexuality.

This book is about God's extreme makeover of me—of my heart. It is my spiritual journey through the heartache and pain and growth and healing of my issues with homosexuality. It is about the slow unraveling and breakdown of my family, and the unexpected change and transformation of my heart that takes me from fear and anger to love and respect for the gay community. The journey has tested me and twisted me and humbled me and broken me. It has produced a measure of endurance in me and it has increased my faith. Sometimes that happens when the truth comes out.

The apostle Paul wrote to the Philippians, "I want you to know, friends, that what has happened to me has really served to advance the gospel and others have been encouraged to speak the word of God more courageously and fearlessly" (Phil. 1:12-14). If this is how it works—that I tell my story and the gospel is advanced and others are encouraged and built up in their faith—then I have written this book with that hope and purpose. I have written for families and other loved ones of those living homosexually who are looking for support; I have written for churches and their congregations who are known by their love; and I have written for the gay community, who deserve my love and respect.

Dr. Nancy Heche
Chicago, Illinois
February 2006

＊　　＊　　＊　　＊

June 2005

I have just finished speaking before an audience of about a thousand people. They are gathered here by a shared experience—the need to process and live with the news of a loved one's homosexuality, and to get resources, support and direction. Some of these people are angry, some are hurting, some are still reeling—many are in pain. As I walk down the platform steps, the crowd is now standing, clapping, sharing comments with their neighbors, checking the agenda for the workshop sessions to follow. Some are smiling at me, some catch my eye and silently mouth "Thank you." Some rush to me and exclaim, "That helps me a lot. Thanks for sharing your story."

An attractive woman approaches me from the midst of others who are leaving the auditorium. No smile—her jaw set, her eyes sad. She reaches for my hands and says, "My husband just left me for another man. I haven't told anyone. We were married for 25 years, like you. What am I going to do?" She is filled with the hurt and fear and anger I recognize so well.

I can only stand there with her, almost 25 years after the same devastating outrage in my own life and shake my head in disbelief. No matter how many times I hear this story, I can't believe it. "I am so sorry," I say to her, a weak response to such intense pain. Somehow we have survived the betrayal—she for a few days, I for a few years. That is the best hope I can give her—I have been through the fire and am here to say that I've made it through another day.

"Can you tell me what happened?" I ask her. Sometimes the telling—and the hearing—of the story creates a connection that comforts us. We are not alone.

We slip through the crowd to a place in the sun and release our broken hearts. We heal, word by word, hand in hand, friend to friend.

＊　　＊　　＊　　＊

CHAPTER 1

Ruin

February 1983

We are eager, even hopeful, biding our time in the small, cramped consulting room. My daughter Abigail and I are at Bellevue Hospital in New York City. Tonight we will finally get some answers. Tonight we will know something.

I have been hounding the medical staff for information about my husband, Don. Ask a question, get a non-answer. It has been as frustrating as waiting at a crowded airport for the overdue flight crew to show up. It feels like a conspiracy. I want answers. I want facts. Why all the mystery? I'm trying to make sense out of this scene. Why doesn't someone help me?

The room is cold and unwelcoming. There are no chairs, only a long metal table with some important-looking papers stacked in one corner. No carpet. No Kleenex tissue. Bellevue is for indigents—it's a city hospital. You go there when you have nothing left and nowhere else to go.

He is young, this doctor coming through the open doorway. Unlike some of the others, he has not yet developed a blank, disinterested expression. Actually, he looks baffled—incredulous that he's the one to break the news. I have pressed, even begged for answers during the past year. "Not much is known about your husband's condition," I was told six months ago. "It doesn't seem to pose a threat to family members," someone else said. "The prognosis is clearly not good. Maybe a year," they offer.

Somewhere down the hall, Don is lying in a ward, demented—in and out of delusions like a man on morphine. He fears the "Continental Army" is coming to get him. I have no idea what else seems real to him by now.

The doctor clears his throat as he picks up a folder from the table and opens it. He glances down, then at me, then at Abigail, then back to me.

"Hasn't anyone told you, Mrs. Heche?" he says. "Your husband is dying of AIDS. He was diagnosed more than a year ago."

The three of us wait in silence. We do not move. His words hardly register. Then Abigail, barely above a whisper, says: "Oh, I think there was an article in *People* magazine about that, just a couple weeks ago."

I do not speak. I *cannot* speak. I push from my mind the *New York Times* magazine story I had read the previous Sunday. AIDS is unfamiliar to the world at this time. It is a dark mystery to us.

My mind begins to reel. Just a year ago, Don and I were still living together. He wasn't always well, but we didn't know what was wrong. He needed surgery in his groin. Spots developed on his arm. White stuff covered his tongue. All I could think at that time was, *Can't you just get your act together so we can get on with our lives?!*

Years later, people would ask me how I could not have known. "You didn't know because you didn't want to know," they said. But it wasn't that simple. It may have been naiveté; it may have been innocence. Admit it Nancy—you're a 50s girl. You grew up with Donna Reed, *Leave It to Beaver*, Doris Day and fairy tales like "Singin' in the Rain." Fairy tales were commonplace in your world—everybody was supposed to live happily ever after. Certainly *I* was supposed to.

For me, I fall in love only to see it all fall apart.

Now in the hospital it all begins to click. The dots connect like an ignited stick of dynamite—the fuse sizzling toward explosion. I realize that I have been lied to my entire married life. Betrayed. Deceived. Abandoned. Emotions rush through me like an electric shock.

Why weren't we enough for him?

What's wrong with us?

He could have been home with his wife and four beautiful children, but instead he was out with a thousand men. Didn't we matter at all?

I am so angry.

I leave the consulting room to call my husband's sister. She has worried about his mysterious poor health also. "I'm not going to do anything with the body," I scream into the phone. "You can have him."

I hate him. I absolutely hate him. I am furious. All I had ever wanted to be was a wife and mother. Now I'm alone. My life will never be the same: I've lost my past as well as my future. He has destroyed our lives—ruined them slowly and secretly, year after year.

He always seemed so confident. So charming. So respected. So *good*. He taught Bible studies, for Pete's sake! He led Sunday School classes. He played the organ and directed the choir, rehearsed our children for the Sunday night church service. *This can't be true.*

Most people I know do not rig their lives in two directions. They integrate life and faith and family. They have a 9 to 5 job, some money in the bank. I remember a line from *The Prince of Tides* when Tom Wingo, the narrator, says: "There are families who live out their entire lives without a single thing of interest happening to them—I've always envied them." I know exactly what he means. I envy those people too.

My family always lived on the edge—the edge of financial security, of job security, marriage security, health security. I longed for a life without a single thing of interest happening to us. I wanted a steady paycheck, a regular job and even an occasional visit to a marriage counselor. Surely those simple things would have solved our problems. I never looked for my husband's kind of excitement—where checks bounce, cars get repossessed, electricity gets turned off, the sheriff blusters his way to our front door, the landlord hauls our furniture onto the boardwalk.

"Well, at least life isn't boring," Don would say with a shrug and a smile.

Right.

We lived blindly and willingly with his desperate addictions—his deep pain. These things I know years later, but not now.

I do not see him that night in the hospital—the night when Abigail and I hear the news. The next day I take my Series Seven exam to become a stockbroker. (Life goes on.) I will steel myself. I am resolute, undefended. Don can go to hell for all I care. I am the family provider now. Forget him.

*   *   *   *

April 1997—14 years since Don's death from AIDS

We have picked up our lives—Abigail, Susan (my oldest daughter), Anne (my youngest daughter) and I. We moved to Chicago shortly after Don died to be closer to Susan, her husband, Jud, and their young son, Elliot.

My condominium home overlooks beautiful Lake Michigan. The seventh-floor vantage point allows a magnificent view and a warm setting for my counseling practice. I've left the world of finance and have earned my master's degree in counseling. I am standing in the kitchen this early spring evening, leaning against the sink with a quick cup of soup, waiting for my next appointment.

Five minutes 'til seven. My client is due at seven. The phone rings. I put my cup on the empty counter and reach for the phone, expecting the receptionist downstairs to say my client is here. I am overjoyed to hear Anne's voice instead. Our connections are brief and over too soon. She has moved beyond dinner theaters and soap operas and is a film and television actress now, living in Hollywood.

Anne is friendly but quick. "Hi, Mom. I'm calling to tell you that I've fallen in love—with a woman. It just happened, last week at the Oscars. But it's real, and it's wonderful. I wanted to tell you right away because it's going to be very public. I know this is probably a real surprise to you, Mom." And then she says good-bye, we'll talk later, she needs to leave for somewhere in a hurry.

I am left standing in the kitchen with the phone in my hand. I can hear the dial tone and then the automated voice. "If you would like to make a call, please hang up and try again." In less than 30 seconds, I am plummeted into disbelief and outrage. I am dumbfounded—in a state of shock.

Doesn't Anne remember what homosexuality has done to our family? I was convinced that it was the whole homosexual world that had torn our family apart. They left us homeless, broken, vulnerable. Did Anne *forget?!* How could she do this?

I have little recollection of what happened during the next hour in the counseling session. My client comes. She talks. She leaves. All I want is to finish the session so that I can call Abigail and Susan.

Finally, I am alone. I walk to the phone, trembling. I wonder, *Will I ever eat another bite of food? Will I ever close my eyes and sleep again?* Maybe if I lie facedown, the knot in my stomach will go away. I don't want to see anyone—I won't be able to keep my pain from leaking onto them. *Will I be able to say Anne's name out loud again? Will friends and even strangers look right through me and see that the scab has been ripped off my deepest wound?* Maybe I'll get a whole new batch of friends so that my old ones won't have to feel sorry for me one more time. "You need to write a book!" they'll say once again. "You're like a present-day Job," they will remind me.

Why can't I just disappear?

The next morning, I trudge from my sunless bedroom to my reading corner on the leather sofa in the living room. Can I even think about this? I am at my wit's end. I pick up my Bible and begin to read and pray. *This will not end in death,* I read, *It is for God's glory so that God's Son may be glorified through it.*[1] Oh, really? When? How? It sure feels like death. If I ask more questions will I get more answers? I can't hear God. Can He hear me? There is no tablet carved in stone delivered from mountain's height, no smoke and rumblings. What should I do? Where can I go? I am finished. Can anything I do or say really change anything that God will do or say? This morning He is far, far away.

What I need is resurrection. Transformation. A new life. *Another* life. I want to board one of those luxury tour buses that lines up at the classy old Drake Hotel on Oak Street. I want to sink into the high front seat where I can stare the world away through dark-tinted windows and be driven to someplace that's not exotic. I want to wave good-bye to me.

Ellen DeGeneres has not "come out" on her weekly sitcom, but there's a buzz that soon it will be written into one of the segments of the show. My daughter will be Ellen's lover, not "outed" on television, but in real life. This morning I am caught by the shock of what that means. With Don, it was all about denial. With Anne, it's all about full disclosure. Don Heche was about secrecy; Anne Heche is about honesty. The secrecy didn't kill Don, the sex did. What price honesty?

Anne's newfound lesbian love affair is like a betrayal of an unspoken vow: *We will never have anything to do with homosexuals.* I had made the assumption that we were all in agreement about this. I do not even say the word "homosexual." I must protect myself—protect my family. Homosexuality has done us wrong.

I try to figure it out. *If Anne embraces Ellen, she'll embrace her father. If she leads his life, she'll connect with him.* Or she'll get some of the love and affection she missed from me, or her sisters, or her father. Or she'll explore a different kind of sex, or . . . or . . . honestly, I don't know.

I get up and go to the window. The sky is streaked with clouds, and the lake is as blue as the heavens. I am desperate for God to say something more. Was this part of His plan to prosper me, to make me more like Jesus? *What do You have to say about this?* I ask Him. *What could You possibly have up Your Holy Sleeve that will convince me that You know what is going on?* I open my Bible to listen. I am ready.

*   *   *   *

Present day

I spend some of my weekends speaking at a faith-based national conference called *Love Won Out,* where psychologists, teachers and researchers share information and personal stories with the audience about their experiences with homosexuality. We go to different cities around the United States and are welcomed by congregations composed of both friends and strangers. There are people on the ultra right who are hoping we will condemn those who are living homosexually. There are others with more liberal views who are hoping we will endorse homosexuality. And always there are the protesters with their angry voices and big cards: JESUS LOVES US TOO ♥!

Parents want to talk about their struggles. They raise their questions in the workshops and in the hallways.

Should the kids stay at our house and sleep together?

What about same-sex weddings?

How do we talk to our other children about this?

How do we talk to our church about this?

What about grandchildren? Family reunions?

When I finish speaking, there are usually several people wanting to talk—parents, kids, friends, disappointed lovers. They tell me their stories—beautiful, sad, heartbreaking stories. One particular afternoon, two women nudge their way to the front of the church to expose some fragments of their broken lives. They share the same shock—beautiful daughters who are lesbians. They tell me about a difficult dinner conversation when their daughters suddenly turned to them in rage and bombarded them with one question after another. "How would you vote on same-sex marriage? And would you allow gays to preach in your church—or even allow them to walk through the door of your holier-than-thou church? When are you ever going to get with it and come into the twenty-first century? You and Dad and your friends make me sick."

"What can we say to them?" the mothers ask me.

Ninety percent of the people I talk to are trying to connect with their children who have "come out." They want their children to know they are loved; they want to maintain a relationship with them, to keep an active interest in their children's lives, even though they may not agree with how they act or what they believe. We try to gain some insight about how to do this with love and respect.

Judy, Houston, tells me about her 18-year-old son who came home late one Saturday night. Her biggest fear was that he was sleeping with his girlfriend—he had been raised to wait until marriage to have sex. This particular Saturday night she waits up for him. She confronts him, hoping to ease her fears. He looks at her with disbelief and anger—with scorn. "You have no idea what I do," he says. The truth is, he's been having a sexual relationship with his best boyfriend since they were both 14. His father hears the commotion downstairs. When he learns what has just transpired, he is ignited with pain and fury. "Get out of my house and never come back!" he explodes.

Marge's 19-year-old daughter just started a new job. Her female boss was helping her move into her new place. "Don't worry, I'll take good care of her," the boss told Marge. The real story leaks out. They are a couple. The boss is more than twice the daughter's age—married, with grown children.

Maria's Hispanic family is proud, traditional. Her husband is petrified that people will find out about their daughter. (I get it. For seven years I kept our secret. I didn't tell anyone that my husband had died of AIDS.) Maria had tried for months to contact her daughter. When her daughter finally e-mailed directions to her house, Maria discovered that the address she had been given was a vacant lot.

Over and over again I hear the same questions of confusion and pain: What did we do wrong? How could we have been better parents? What do we do now? How do we act around them? What do we say?

I have no easy answers for those who share their stories with me. But I can tell them about how God is changing me, winning me over to love. Maybe that will give them hope. What I have come to realize is that my journey is not about figuring out or changing anyone else. It's about changing me. It's about moving from the agonizing domination of fear and anger to the blessed realm of love and respect.

Myla Goldberg writes about Saul, the father in her popular book *Bee Season*, "Saul's heart is so full of love that he can feel his eyes fill with it, can feel love dripping down his cheeks." I want to be full of love like that!

So many times I have wanted to love—to be loving toward others. Instead I hold on to what I think is my right to feel hurt, misunderstood, betrayed. I carry the heavy weight of self-righteousness and an entitlement to be right—"You should have . . ." "How *could* you?" "Don't ever . . ."—imagining that I could deliver some punishment or inflict some pain on them that would awaken them to the hurt I feel and thereby compel *them* to change. I brood over the injustice and cruelty of it all—whatever *it* is. I do not love them. I hold a grudge, refuse to engage or interact. I slam down the phone. Even if I have said the words "I love you," it's obvious to them and to everyone else that I do not.

Why is it so hard? Because it's about giving it up, laying it down, letting it go, surrendering all. And what I'm giving up is *me,* what I'm laying down is *my* way, what I'm surrendering is my right to be right, to have it all, to have it all right now.

At the end of the day, I must love. I must bless. I must believe. The apostle Paul's thoughts in 1 Corinthians 13 echo through me:

"Nancy, when you speak, people will put their fingers in their ears and go 'lalalalala' if you don't have love."

"Nancy, you can get your academic degrees and know a little bit about a lot of things, but it means nothing without love."

"Nancy, you can win the lottery and give it all away, but it means nothing without love."

"It's not about how much you say or how much you know or how much you do; it's about how much you love."

I *know* this! So just do it, Nancy. Love. *You* change.

The rest of this story is my journey to that place.

CHAPTER 2

Hints

My family never talked about anything when I was growing up.

More accurately, we never talked about anything *except* politics. Even as an adult, I remember sitting at the dining room table, all eyes on my father at the head of the table, trying to keep my eyes open as he droned on and on about political issues and personalities. After he served the pot roast and potatoes and carrots, he had a captive audience.

Couldn't he tell that no one was listening? Couldn't he see that we didn't really care about that?

The life-changing, life-threatening conversations that needed to be discussed were avoided; truth got distorted, feelings ignored. Would it have been so hard for my parents to say or at least hint at the important issues? "Nancy, we've seen Don in a car with that character across the street. You know, he lives alone and doesn't have a very good reputation." Hint, hint.

Or, "Girls, I'm going to stay in Washington for longer periods of time, and you and your mother will stay in Albion. She and I are going to take some time away from each other." Hint, hint.

Or, "Nancy, we're very concerned about you and Don. You're much too young to think about getting married. You should be dating lots of people. You mustn't spend so much time alone, especially in his car." Hint, hint.

I can think of all the times that I was oblivious to what was going on around me, to all the things I missed that could have prepared me for what was ahead. Blink once and miss a seductive glance; blink twice and miss the whole affair.

My sister, Penny, and I are identical twins, the only children of our late parents, Richard and Susan Prickett. My father owned and published a weekly newspaper in Albion, Indiana. He had printer's ink in his veins, and he loved politics. He wrote his way from Albion all the way to Capitol Hill, where he worked as a speechwriter and campaign manager for three men in Congress.

Our family commuted between Albion and Washington, D.C., for several years when my father ran the campaign at home during election time and wrote letters and speeches in Washington when Congress was in session. When it was time for Penny and me to begin high school, my mother and my sister and I stayed in Albion, where my mother ran the printing business. My father stayed in Washington, where he conducted his "monkey business."

That arrangement was my first introduction to the deception and betrayal that would storm my own family. Somewhere in the midst of his long commutes, my father began his clandestine extramarital affairs. He was already gone a lot, and now he became totally useless. There were more long periods of silence, blindness, truth distorted, feelings ignored and a marriage and family almost destroyed. But the feelings of loss and shame are stored in my bones. I cannot forget. The scepter of betrayal and deception got passed to my own family.

Two unspoken rules plagued us: *Don't ask questions* and *Don't discuss feelings.* The rules created a mandate of silence. This patriarchal system produced an illusion of power and an environment of intimidation. Did I have an opinion? Did I have an idea? Did I disagree? It didn't matter. I had no power and no access to the power. Did I suspect something? (Don't ask. Don't say a word. Close your eyes, turn away, and act as if nothing has happened.) Did I feel frightened, insecure, lonely, sad, angry, exuberant? "Settle down." That's what I heard. "Settle down." I had no voice. It seemed as if I didn't matter at all. A few unforgettable incidents prolonged the plague and exposed how our family system worked.

* * * *

Because of our involvement with our church youth group, my sister and I were chosen to go to a summer ecumenical conference for high school leaders at Lake Geneva, Wisconsin. "It's a real honor," Rev. Doyle told me. (Our new minister was eager to get his church members involved in new activities.) "You'll meet kids from all across the country. And you'll get some fresh ideas for our church."

This was the same summer I had met Don, and although I really liked him, when I got to Lake Geneva, I found my eyes wandering to a cute blond guy from Detroit. He had a tougher, more rugged look than Don, broad-shouldered and about six and half feet tall—well maybe not quite that tall! His eyes wandered to me, too, and we spent all our free time together. "Let's have lunch in the dining hall at 12:20. The crowd will have cleared out," he teased.

Okay!

"I'll meet you on the beach right before dinner when everyone else is back in their cabins getting showered."

Okay!

Innocent flirtations, seductive winks, warm hand-holding. *Maybe I need to keep my options open!*

"C'mon, Nance, I'll carry you up the hill so we don't miss the burgers and fries."

Okay!

My tall, blond guy carried me in his arms like a baby, huffing and puffing all the way to the top of the hill, laughing and nuzzling.

"Oh, you are so strong!" I cooed.

At the end of the conference, along with his good-bye kiss, he asked me to come to his high school graduation the following spring. "Oh, you're a senior!" I could go for this older man!

We wrote to each other and talked on the phone a few times during his senior year, still planning my trip to Detroit for his graduation. This was, of course, all hidden from Don, who had become my steady boyfriend back home. But our family was in Washington by the time Detroit's graduation rolled around, so I was able to keep this romance a secret!

My father had hinted that I could go. I was sure that my enthusiasm would win my father's final approval. After all, my parents wanted me to date some guys other than just Don. Here was their opportunity to practice what they preached.

I can still see my father at his cluttered desk in his impressive office in the Old House Office Building on Capitol Hill that sad, infuriating day when he said I couldn't go to the graduation. No discussion. No questions. No comments. It seemed as if I didn't matter at all.

Another humiliating event centered on a potential boyfriend, this time from my own school. He was a year older, with sparkling, mischievous dark eyes, and he rode a motorcycle! To be asked on a date with him was a coveted prize. There were a lot of girls who flirted with him between classes, and he flirted right back. I knew *nothing* about teenage male hormones. I thought dates were about holding hands (maybe), and laughing, having fun, cokes, movies, a goodnight kiss. Is that what he was thinking when he invited me to a concert in Ft. Wayne, the big city almost an hour away? I thought so. I was ecstatic and naive.

My father just said, "No. You can't go to the concert with him." No discussion. No questions. No comments. What were my father's concerns and feelings? About me? About the boy? Why wouldn't he talk to me about his concerns?

But we never talked about anything.

*   *   *   *

A few years ago, I let myself express my anger to my mother about what I thought was her neglect and disregard for one of my grandchildren, her great-grandchild. I let it all out. I cried and screamed and scolded. Of course my anger wasn't only about what happened with my grandchild, it was about me, about some old hurts I had never discussed or healed or forgiven. It was about all the times I had felt neglected and ignored, all the times I didn't seem to matter.

My mother didn't get it. She just froze. "STOP IT!" she said, glaring at me. "Your father used to get emotional like that, and I didn't know what to do with him either. Settle down."

No further discussion.

When I graduated from high school, I was chosen as class Salutatorian. I thought it was an honor for our family as well as for me. I don't remember if my parents congratulated me. But I do remember that my twin sister was not told about the selection process or the result. I don't even know when or how she eventually found out. I wonder what mysterious disadvantage my parents thought would befall my sister if she were informed and allowed to celebrate with me.

Graduation night came. All 48 seniors marched from the back of the high school gym dressed in blue and white caps and gowns to the familiar ceremonial "Pomp and Circumstance." A lot of pomp for our small-town band of seniors.

I gave my speech and then it was over—just another chapter in the Prickett family history, recorded without words or emotion, without acknowledgment or fanfare.

*   *   *   *

Sometimes we still don't discuss the issues, the struggles, the negotiations, the reconciliations. Hidden ledgers of unpaid debts keep us in bondage to each other: "You should have . . ." "Why didn't you . . .?" "You never . . ." My anger binds me to my mother. I cater to my legacy. I don't talk to her.

The heavy circular door revolves, and some of my children do not speak to each other.

"What you don't forgive you pass on," Bob Sears, my therapist, confided. I have so wanted to figure this out so that I don't pass it on—my resentment, my hurt, my anger. I'm too late for some of it. My daughters Susan and Abigail did not watch Anne on her soap opera; Abigail and Anne did not read Susan's published book; Anne and Susan did not celebrate Abigail's return to college. No one cracked open a bottle of champagne in my new office at the bank. My mother pretended that the lives portrayed in Susan's book did not exist. We're all invisible to each other. We can make it on our own. We do not—we cannot—get too close. We don't connect. *Please,* graft me into an Italian family!

The sins of the father and the mother visit the children—"But they don't have to live there," Susan wrote in her book *Anonymity*. So our lives are changing; what didn't happen in my family of origin is now happening with my grandchildren. We talk. We listen. We ask. We discuss, look, see and hear it all. We say that we are special, loved, valued. I try to celebrate and acknowledge everything they do.

Two of my grandchildren, Natalie and Bennet, who are 17 and 13, were recently scheduled to sing in the talent show at their school. I had to be out of town. But, oh, how I wanted to hear their music! So we set up a private concert before I left for my trip. Abigail arranged it all. Elise, my oldest granddaughter, was home from college. It was a family affair. Elise, Abigail and I sat cross-legged on Natalie's bedroom floor, eyes and attention riveted on the talented teenage performers. Ben played his guitar, and he and Natalie sang together. Awesome! Then we clapped and raved and begged for more. Lots of celebration and adoration! I weep today when I think about that moment—sealed in time. How cherished and celebrated the words and music, and the children more precious than life!

A lack of emotional openness, and presence and celebration, is not something I could know or describe as a child; but the pervasive feelings of abandonment and brokenness took root in my heart. What could save me from those feelings—from my family? As a high school graduate, I thought I knew. What I needed was to be swept away by an unsuspecting blond, blue-eyed, crew-cut, eyes-wide-open Prince Charming into a land of authenticity and honesty. That would solve everything, wouldn't it? Wait and see . . .

*   *   *   *

When I was 15, an energetic young minister and his family came to our church, appointed by the District Superintendent of the Warsaw District of the Methodist Church. It was a big deal. We had survived the faithful Rev. Beale, but we welcomed Rev. Doyle with the enthusiasm and relief of teenagers who knew a better thing when we saw it. He started a youth group that became the turning point for my spiritual life. I didn't know very much about God, but I was excited to get involved in the youth group. I wanted to be religious, whatever that meant. In my graduation speech, I wanted to witness to my newfound religion. "Behold, I stand at the door and knock," I said, a zealous preacher in tasseled cap and gown on the stage of the high school gym. It seemed like the perfect Bible verse—the only one I knew, actually. I boldly presented it to the seniors who were starting a new life. I felt passionate about encouraging others to give "religion" a chance. It was new to me and seemed like a good thing. My heart was yearning for something more—maybe their hearts were, too, and would follow me if I extended the invitation.

This church youth group became the venue that drew Don and me together when we were 16 years old. It was May 1953. He was the fair-haired boy playing the organ at the regional youth rally in Mentone, Indiana. It was my first excursion with Rev. Doyle and the youth group, as well as an introduction to a whole new world of other high school kids who were interested in religion (or maybe new boyfriends or girlfriends). Whatever the reason, it brought us to a small town in the Midwest and to a white frame church with rows of wooden pews on worn oak floors to sing and hear an inspiring speaker.

But in that sanctuary full of 150 kids and their preacher chaperones, the world narrowed to Don and me. He was proud, skillful, an insider in this new appealing world, and friendly with my Rev. Doyle. (I secretly hoped that the friendship would parlay into an introduction for me with Don.) Don's hands flew up and down the keys; his stocking feet danced on the pedals close to the floor. He was good, really good.

Give me oil in my lamp. Keep me burning, burning, burning.
Give me oil in my lamp, I pray.
And *Kum baya, My Lord, Kum baya.*
I knew I had to meet this cute guy.

Rev. Doyle had introduced him at the beginning of the meeting and played with his name—Heche—with a joke about how it sounded kind of like a sneeze and rhymed with the letter "H" with a little breath in front of it. I said his name slowly in my heart—H-ayt-ch. I will never forget how to pronounce that name, I vowed quietly. After the rally, I walked right over to the crowd around him and flirted with a perky "Hi!"

Don was dating another girl at the time—how I acquired that bit of gossip so early in the game only another teenager in love will tell you. But about a month later, June 9, we met again at the church camp for future leadership candidates in the Methodist Church. This time Don walked over to me and smiled. "Want to run around together?" was his invitation.

Lucky me. I kissed him after the bonfire that first night. *This is the beginning of a beautiful love story,* I wrote in my diary.

Don's family lived in the back of the small grocery store owned and run by his parents, Joe and Clara, or more accurately, owned and run by his mom. Don's father was a bum. He was unshaven and reeked of beer and cigarettes—the classic profile of the father of a homosexual man, as I learned much later. Don's mom was pleasant but stressed by her hard work and hard life. She was always rushing, running back and forth from the meat cooler to the candy case to the cash register, waiting on customers and making excuses for Joe. "He's in the back . . ."

My mother's feeble concession, as she desperately looked for a way to allow herself—and me—contact with this "backwater" family, as she put it, was that they had a "gold mine" in their summer-resort gas station and grocery store business. I wondered if she was talking herself or me into believing this was a rich family, a suitable family. She wanted me to marry a millionaire. "It's just as easy to fall in love with a rich man as a poor man," she hinted.

In spite of my mother's small-town simplicity, she had a measure of perceived sophistication derived from our stint in Washington and our Quaker heritage. But this was not her idea of a good match. That didn't matter. I had come too far to turn back now. All of the opportunities for questions and discussions had been missed. Remember our family: We didn't talk about anything. We didn't ask questions and we didn't discuss feelings. It was too late to begin now.

I would make this decision with my heart, on my own.

If Don's home environment troubled him, he didn't show it to me. We were having too much fun, always on the go—basketball games in the

winter, more youth meetings and rallies, movies and drive-ins in the summer, high school plays and dances. We learned to jitterbug in my parents'
kitchen, rocking and rolling like every '50s couple in love. Don was a great
dancer, and we crashed every neighboring high school prom—white dinner jacket for him, strapless gown for me. We were the "cute couple" that
friends nominated as King and Queen on the radio request show on
Saturday mornings, and "Most Likely to Succeed" in the school popular-
ity contest.

We parked and necked in Don's '52 Chevy coupe, but never talked about
sex. Nobody did, at least not my friends or family. My parents rarely discussed sex with me, and when they did, it was so vague and awkward and
strange, like a new language, that I didn't know what they meant.

"I know you don't believe me, but I had feelings just like you do," my
mother would hint.

What do you mean? No one *ever* felt the way I do!

"Be careful. You remember what happened to that girl in the seventh
grade," my father warned in a rare family meeting.

But what is it that I'm supposed to be so careful about?

I doubt that I ever heard the word "homosexual." And I certainly
didn't know any homosexuals. Or if I did, I would have been positive that
they lived a long way from Albion, Indiana.

My parents knew some homosexuals though, or at least they knew of
them. Of course they didn't talk about them. Years after Don died, my
mother raised her eyebrows in a knowing kind of way when she reminded
me that our church organist lived with another man. (Hint, hint.) All
through high school, I simply thought they were roommates—you know,
like people who share rooms at college. Don seemed friendly toward them.
I just thought it was the music thing they had in common. Anyway, Don
was friends with everybody. And I was clueless.

There was a guy in Don's high school class who acted a little weird.
He was flamboyant and effeminate, hard to take, but irresistibly engaging
and creative. He designed a ridiculous "Trojan Horse" costume—the team
was the North Webster Trojans—that fit over his head and body and that
he wore at the basketball games. He romped along the bleachers, mane

and tail flying, head wobbling up and down. You couldn't help but laugh. He was Don's buddy. I thought Don was being nice to him—everyone else tried to ignore him. I learned not long ago that he died of AIDS. I don't know what his friendship with Don was like, but then again, I never asked.

It's hard to be suspicious when you're dating the North Webster High School superstar. Don was Mr. Everything—Mr. Charming, Mr. Talent, Mr. Brains. Popular and smart, he starred in basketball, music and academics. I had no reason not to trust him. *Don't ask, don't tell*—we practiced this long before the military did.

One Saturday night—date night in the winter, because basketball was Friday night—he showed up for a date with a black eye. He looked shaken, a little pale. Usually he was so tan that, with his sun-bleached hair, he looked almost like a black-and-white photographic negative—really tanned skin and really light hair.

He smiled his charm and charisma right onto my mouth when he kissed me hello. Seemed okay to me! But his father had gone on a drinking binge, he said, swearing, shouting, throwing things around their store. Having a father who was distant and unavailable is one thing; but having a father who beats you and your mother is another. When he had seen his father grab his mother, crash her against the store displays and then push her into the ice cream case, Don leveled his father. Or maybe Don's dad leveled him. But that was the end of the story. The tale was told. There were no further comments or questions. We didn't talk about anything either.

* * * *

It has taken more than 20 years for me to muster any compassion for Don. Once, shortly after his horrible double life was exposed, somebody said, "Your husband must have been in a lot of pain." I retorted, "I hope so." I have been so angry over the years. The lies. The fraud. The destruction of our home and family. The ongoing consequences of brokenness and loss.

Kate, the stalwart girlfriend and eventual wife portrayed in the movie *The Family Man,* foresees a bright future for her and Jack right now, right where they are, rather than waiting a year while Jack takes advantage of a great business opportunity in London. "It's just a year," he promises. "Then I'll be back."

"I choose us," Kate says. "Right now, right here, Jack." She reaffirms it later in the scene when he's ready to move to the city, uproot their lives and leave their familiar suburban home and friends and family. "I choose us."

I hear those words and recoil. Why? Because I am one of the millions of spouses who was not chosen. Memories of deception and false hope and disillusionment dart through my mind. My eyes fill with tears and my throat aches with grief when I hear those words. I feel resentful and defensive. Why wasn't I chosen? Why wasn't I enough? Why wasn't I smart enough to make it work? Why didn't I see it coming?

"You didn't ask the hard questions," people scold. "Deep down you really didn't want to know. You closed your eyes and looked the other way. Maybe you knew and pretended you didn't. You were probably living in denial."

That's right. I didn't want to know that my husband was fornicating with other men in bathhouses and men's rooms and hotel rooms and party rooms all around the country under the guise of traveling for business. I didn't want to know that I wasn't chosen, even though I felt neglected and abandoned and disconnected. I didn't want to think about all the consequences and complications and pain.

Why would I want to find out that awful truth? What would I do if I did know? What *could* I do? They're right—I didn't want to know. What would I do with the information? I was a wife and mother. That was my job—the only one I ever wanted. Who gets paid for that job? Where would we go? How would we survive? How could I bear the truth that we were not chosen. Wife *and* children—and he would not choose us? I couldn't bear knowing it.

But of course I did find out. I do know now. We all know. I never heard him say, "I choose us." He chose a secret bisexual life that left us drowning in debt, sinking in emotional pain and immersed in grief and loss and confusion.

People ask me how Don could have kept his double life a secret from me for so long. (For 25 years we never spoke about his homosexuality.)

It was easy. Patterns of secrecy and denial are repeated. Just as Don learned to keep his father's violence and alcoholism a secret, he learned to keep his same-sex attraction and struggle secret, maintaining the system of denial and discretion that was required to hold body and soul together during high school, college and then marriage.

It was easy for me too. Remember, I had grown up with "Don't ask questions; don't discuss feelings." Just close your eyes. Turn away. Blink once. Blink twice. Silence and blindness, secrecy and denial were not new to me. It took a doctor at Bellevue Hospital to open my eyes, to speak the truth and reveal my husband's dirty secret.

Oh, sure, there were hints—the funny way Don flipped his wrist sometimes when he was laughing; his quirky walk; his obsession with style and awareness of fashion—clothes, hair, furniture, flowers, make-up—glaring red flags obvious to everybody 20 years later in a culture where homosexuality and the gay culture are around every corner. If only I had known then what I know now. But I was plagued by my past and by the disaster-producing rules that were ingrained in me. *Don't ask questions. Don't discuss feelings.* I was a perfect candidate for the wife of a man who lived a double life.

Part of my continuing healing comes in learning to forgive my late husband—to understand that the things he dealt with were so much deeper than he or I could have imagined. His father never attended a basketball game or school play or concert, never had even one man-to-man conversation with his son, never affirmed Don's masculinity. Don had one sister, who was 19 years older, so he was virtually raised as an only child by a ruling mother and an abusive father.

*   *   *   *

There is a lot of talk today about whether homosexuals are "born that way" or "choose that way." The climate in Don's home was perfect for a deeply wounded young man to "choose that way." The environment modeled neither a healthy heterosexual marriage nor a positive role model from either parent. As I began to recognize these facts, as I began to understand a small part of what he went through, what names he had been called, what wounds he had suffered—as I was willing to imagine the world through Don's eyes—I started my journey from shock, shame, fear and anger to love and respect.

I don't mean to imply that one's family environment is responsible for one's homosexuality. I don't blame Don's parents for his sexual choices. But they were responsible for their drunkenness and violence, for their dominance and overprotection. He was responsible for the choices he made, and he bore (and we still bear) the consequences.

I wish his parents had paid attention to him, had talked with him—just as I wish my parents had paid attention to me and talked with me. If my parents had done that, maybe I would have learned to pay attention. Maybe I would have learned how to ask questions. Maybe I would have been more aware of what was going on around me. But hindsight, as they say, is always 20/20. My responsibility now is to change my unhealthy habits. Ask the hard questions. Open my eyes. Look around. Pay attention.

*   *   *   *

My son-in-law Jud pays attention. He has a heart governed by thoughtfulness, gentleness and love. He possesses an awareness that keeps him present and available.

Last year, in late summer, Jud, Susan, Bennet and I sat on the patio at their home in Barrington, Illinois. Suddenly, Jud started from his chair. "Listen! I hear the sandhill cranes—this is their migration time," he announced. "Let's go!" He motioned for us to get up and follow him as he took off running. I knew this was something he would not let us miss.

Jud knows things. He yelled over his shoulder as we chased him across the lawn, "The sandhills were once nearly extinct in the Midwest. They've made a comeback now and we can catch a glimpse of them in the marsh if we hurry. Look for the spot of red on the top of their heads."

We ran looking up, hoping to see Jud's treasure in the sky, and strain-
ing to hear him, not wanting to lose a word of what he was saying.
He slowed down so that we could join him.

"The sandhills begin their exodus in Michigan and fly to southeast-
ern Georgia and Florida to wait out the winter," he said. "Sometimes they
stop in our marsh. They can fly at 50 miles per hour and cover nearly 500
miles in one day. After struggling and spiraling up to 12,000 or 15,000
feet, they may sail for long periods on set wings, riding the thermals until
they're out of view against the horizon."

It was these magnificent birds—something beautiful and wonderful and worthy of notice—to which Jud opened our eyes. "Once a year—
only once—can you get a look at these cranes, and now they have come
right to our property. We must hurry. I can hear them—c'mon, c'mon,"
he urged.

We went around the pond, up the path by the tennis courts and down
to the marsh, pushing tree branches and shoulder-high cattails aside
until the ground began to get muddy and we could go no further without sinking into the marshy wetness.

I was breathless, hopeful. Then I heard it, the sandhills' distinct trum-
peting sound: *garoo-oo-ooo-a-a-a.*

"They have a huge windpipe that they coil into their sternum," Jud
said. "It looks like Elise's French horn, in the pictures I've seen. That's
what creates their loud, distinctive call. That's what I heard on the patio."
Jud continued to share his morsels of information.

But there in the damp marsh grass, having run as far as possible, I got
stuck. I felt light-headed. Would I miss them? I thought, *I came this far, but
I can't get enough height to see the cranes folded down into the tall reeds and rushes.*
I heard them. I was so close. They were so loud! But I can't see them.

Then came a gift. Strong hands. Strong shoulders. Jud, who is 6'2"
with a handsome Swedish build, picked me up, high above the marsh
foliage, so that I could see the birds. They are wading and feeding, as
comfortable and regal as kings in a swampy castle.

This is Jud's pleasure. He simply could have known about the sandhills and chosen to ignore them, and us. We could have sat lazily on the
patio and listened to his story about these marvelous birds. But this is

Jud. He is attentive, aware. He acknowledges not only the value of the event, but the value of us. He and Susan have created a new pattern of observing, regarding, articulating, discovering.

On this day, I do not look away or close my eyes.

With our hands to our foreheads, eyes open and scanning the horizon, we watched the sandhills fly low over the pond, just high enough to clear the trees. We watched them flap and struggle in their upward spiral until they caught the thermals and disappeared out of sight.

CHAPTER 3

Promises, Promises

I remember the last time I told my husband that I loved him. It was the weighty week before Christmas 1981. We were back from Sunday morning church—well warmed and well inspired. I was sitting sidesaddle on Don's lap in the flowery overstuffed chair in our friend's living room.

This room, this home, this other family had become our family's refuge from the landlord's storm that raged against us for nonpayment of rent. We pretended that all was well. I was settled, cozy and confidant—loved and loving—while Jan balanced the preparation of meat, potatoes and vegetables, and everyone else arranged silverware and paper napkins beside the Fiesta dinner plates in the crowded, sunny dining room. They were willing to double up on chores in order to give Don and me time alone, propping up their hope for us with whispers and smiles.

We all believed that if we did just one more endearing thing—if we served him chastely, loved him blindly—we would save Don and our family, and he would come to his senses and get a job! I was "easy like Sunday mornin'" as the old song invites, loving him, enduring him, waiting and trusting. For better or for worse. "I believe in you. I love you." After a good church service we were at our best. I believed there would be a deal—I'm his wife. That's what I do.

*   *   *   *

It started out so well—1953. Next stop easy street if you make good grades, go to church youth group, star on the basketball team and have a great musical talent. We were from the '50s—Don and I. We could rock 'n' roll with superstar Elvis or croon with the Four Freshmen and Frank Sinatra. We fell in love in the back row at the movies. We closed our eyes and danced cheek to cheek, humming, "They tried to tell us we're 'too young,' too young to really fall in love . . ." Don and I are young, but we're smart and good-looking. That's all it takes, isn't it?

When we're together, we dazzle—teenage prince and princess in a small-town northern Indiana high school kingdom, royalty misplaced and eventually dethroned. We're charming and attractive, excelling in all the school contests, starring in the plays and concerts during the school year. Don is the envy of all the other guys; I'm the envy of all the girls.

In the summer, we worked and played at the Epworth Forest campgrounds, the summer home of the Methodist Church Youth Conference in North Webster, Indiana. We were counselors at the junior high camp where the campers staged a mock wedding for Don and me. With Queen Anne's lace chosen from a nearby field to serve as a bouquet, and an old lace curtain scrounged from some musty closet for a veil, I walked the sandy aisle to meet my laughing lifeguard groom. The giddy girls swooned, hoping for a chance to kiss the groom; the bashful boys stood by in wonder.

My mother, who was in the audience as a spectator, scowled her disapproval. "They're making fun of something that may be very serious for you some day," she told me. Little did I know that some of her concern was related to her own marriage that was in serious trouble at the time.

Besides his job as lifeguard for the campers, Don played the rented Hammond organ for the weekly music programs at camp. Anna and Varner Chance were the college music professors who converted teenage campers into choristers. It wasn't just the opportunity to be on stage for the Friday night musical that brought the girls to choir practice every day from noon to one o'clock and made them miss their lunch; they could also be a player in the intricate process that musicians share before a performance. Maybe they would get a solo and get to practice alone with the organist. He was so *cute* and so much fun. (It wasn't all about music.)

I was proud as a peacock. I knew that Don liked me. I had his class ring clearly displayed for all the girls to see. They would quickly glance from my smiling face to my ring finger to see if he was available. And though one guy tried to put his arm around me during the benediction at the end of the concert, and another cornered me in the snack bar at the beach, they did it in vain. I wasn't available either. I was going steady with Don Heche. I was hooked!

Because we wanted to see each other as often as possible, and we didn't attend the same high school; and because he worked long hours at his parents' grocery store to earn money for college, and I had a cool car that I loved to drive, we took turns driving the 18 miles from Albion to North Webster. When I made the last turn so that I could see the backwaters close to the store, and then his house, I hit the accelerator and practically squealed into his driveway. *If he sees me, or hears me, and he's not busy with a customer, he'll run out and kiss me!*

*   *   *   *

I wasn't the only one to recognize Don's exceptional giftedness. As one of five top high-school seniors in the country to receive such an award, Don accepted a full scholarship to Indiana University from General Motors—one more indication of future success.

He started college as a philosophy major, intent on becoming a Methodist minister. I was an elementary education major. By our sophomore year, Don had switched to hospital administration and enrolled in the business school. It's true that a certain amount of indecisiveness is allowed in college, especially in the first couple of years, so I didn't think twice about it.

In his junior year, after the birth of our first child, Don switched again, this time to pre-med. He announced it out of the blue at a freshman orientation meeting where he, as one of the chosen campus leaders, was introducing incoming students to campus life. My mother and I happened to be at that meeting. When we heard him say that he was going into pre-med, we jerked our heads toward each other in shock. My mother's shock turned to delight. She always wanted me to marry a doctor.

My shock turned to shame. I had not heard a word about this until that very moment. It came like a shot. How could I hide my humiliation?

But I was so quick. I was used to finding out things after the fact. I recovered in the blink of an eye. I ignored the pain and got to the other end of the emotional spectrum: All right, I'm thrilled at the thought of being a doctor's wife—my mother had certainly drilled it into me often enough. It meant money, security, prestige—just what we expected. Don probably thought I'd like the surprise.

In his senior year, Don was elected to Phi Beta Kappa, academia's coveted key for highest honors. I was sitting in my senior psychology class and someone called out congratulations to me. "For what?" I said. Then they passed a copy of the campus newspaper to me from the back of the room, and I saw Don's name underlined in the list of four other honorees. Why hadn't we received a personal notice, a phone call, letter or something? Then we realized that most senior pre-med students were in Indianapolis at IU's medical school campus. Because Don had changed majors in his junior year, he was a year late in going off campus to Indianapolis. Still, all signs pointed to sweet success.

*   *   *   *

Don didn't get down on one knee when he asked me to marry him, but the shiny square-cut diamond spoke for itself. He opened the gift, took out the ring and finessed it on to the fourth finger of my left hand, a sure token of his love and a symptom of our innocence and passion.

It was Christmas Eve, 1955, our freshman year of college. We were in my parents' living room, enchanted on the green sectional sofa. Later we floated across the street to St. Mark's Lutheran Church for a midnight Christmas Eve service. Snow sparkled in the streetlights, candles flickered on the altar, Paul Brumbaugh sang "O Holy Night" and the aroma of fresh-cut pine branches filled the festive church. It was Christmas-card perfect. We would both turn 19 in less than three months.

Good news travels fast in Smith, my dorm home away from home at IU in Bloomington. A new year, our second semester, a good time for a welcome-back celebration—and I'm the one celebrated! As the first bride-to-be on the floor, I receive the first fruits. All the girls on the fourth floor take this opportunity to fantasize about being homemakers. By proxy I take delivery of the noisy appliances and decorative home accessories.

The floor buzzes with my wedding plans. Who would I choose as bridesmaids? My sister, Penny, of course; Erlene, my childhood friend, who was ultimately forbidden by her priest to attend the Protestant wedding; Margot, who described things as "lovely"—a word I had never used—and was my best-loved suite-mate from Chicago (50 years later, she is still best loved, though she lives far away); and Shirley, a perky darling and my new best friend from Evansville, Indiana.

Before I had a chance to get down the aisle, Shirley and Elmo, a fraternity brother of Don's, eloped, and Shirley gained the prestige of being the first bride on the floor. No one asked why the hurry for this "high society" couple from southern Indiana. It was just a lot of fun figuring out all the intricacies of sneaking out of the dorm, missing curfew, stuffing her bed with pillows in case there was a bed check. (Remember, this is 1955—there were no co-ed dorms; and there were strict rules and tight discipline for offenders, and lots of questions asked by the dorm mothers.) Don and I were the secret witnesses for Shirley and Elmo, standing beside them like reasonable, romantic grown-ups. A few weeks later, Shirley miscarried.

Soon our wedding plans were in full swing. The invitations were ordered from the catalogs at my father's printing business; handmade mints were selected from Martha's Sweet Shoppe; the wedding cake was to be created by the hometown artist and baker Lois McWilliams. I unveiled my beautiful embroidered organdy wedding dress in Indianapolis one spring outing away from campus.

Don and I were blissful, ecstatic, in love, waiting to make love. And in just a few months, June 10, 1956, all would be possible.

Happy Days in Bloomington: Big Ten basketball, pizza, big bands, cashmere sweaters, saddle shoes, suede jackets, and more love right around the corner. All we had to do was execute finals week. Six days. My final exam, English Literature, was on the last day of finals week, June 4. I wrote a hopeful footnote to the professor on the last page of the nearly blank blue exam booklet: "Please have mercy. I'm getting married in six days." She passed me with a B.

We are ready. Anything we don't know, we don't need to know. We are bold and restless. We are adults now. Sign your name on a marriage license and what's not possible? I wonder if Don breathed a silent sigh of relief when he vowed, "I take you, Nancy, to be my lawful wedded wife, to have and to hold, from this day forward." *Donald, do you promise to love and cherish Nancy and, forsaking all others, keep yourself only unto her as long as you both shall live?* "I do."

What was he thinking? Was marrying me his way out of a fresher passion? Would the forbidden, urgent sex go away if he had a wife? Surely he could control this disorientation once he was married. And no one ever needed to know what happened.

If he gave us a second thought—*Will we be okay? Is she the one for me? Is this the right thing to do?*—he never mentioned it. We had taken a survey for engaged couples in *Ladies' Home Journal* and we scored high—most likely to succeed in marriage.

And what about me? I did give it some thought. I was on the debate team and took the side of "Yes, 18-year-olds are ready for marriage." Please don't laugh. Remember being 18? I knew everything. So did Don. We would be just fine—great, in fact.

I confess that there was one teensy, weensy time when I had a second thought about Don and me. It was the weekend before high school graduation. Our new minister, an alumnus of Asbury College in Kentucky, blessed the congregation with a heavenly treat—his college choir visited our church and sang their way right into my unsuspecting heart. Well, not the whole choir, just the tall, dark, handsome baritone in the back row, right-hand side. I noticed him right away. *How can I make a dent in this man's day?* I wondered.

My father had a new Oldsmobile convertible, light blue with dark blue top, a seductive car. I had the keys. I also had the distinction of being the official hostess for the visitors, because I was president of the youth group. I was the likely one, the obvious one, actually the only one to extend an official, dutiful, generous invitation to the performers, well, at least one of them. Of course, I should do it. "Be my guest? Tour the town in my beautiful blue Oldsmobile?" Timing is everything, and we snuck away like mischievous children, still innocent, my long blonde hair blowing in the wind like a movie star, his smile shining brighter than the May sunshine. *Goodbye, IU. Hello, Asbury. Hello, what's-your-name. Good-bye Don.*

But it was more complicated than that. My father was not about to pay for a private, out-of-state school for me—he was having enough trouble keeping up with his own out-of-state affairs. He said that if I wanted to go to Asbury, I would have to pay for it myself. I had no idea in the world how to make that happen.

I didn't know it at the time, but this was probably one of the biggest decisions my father would ever make on my behalf. This decision shed light on a scriptural principle: "If the owner of the house had known at what time of night the thief was coming, he would have kept watch and would not have let the house be broken into."[1]

I attribute some responsibility (maybe even blame) to my father for his lack of guidance and direction for my future. He was the owner of the house. Since he didn't know when disaster would strike—of course he couldn't see into the future—he needed to keep watch on his family (that's what the Scripture verse implies). My father needed to keep his eyes open for hints and clues, to pay attention to imminent danger. He needed to make decisions, even help his family make decisions that would protect us from the "thief."

I am making a bold accusation here—that if my father had said I could go to Asbury and had himself paid the tuition and room and board—I would have had a completely different life, for sure, and maybe a less tragic one. His refusal to send me to Asbury was not just about my choice of college; it was about my unknown, unguarded future and his secret infidelities.

Although my father is not to blame for my difficult life, I bear the consequences of his neglect. If he had known what the thief would take from his family because of his unfaithfulness—even to the second and third generations—he might have stayed at home and kept watch and not have let the house be broken into.

"Ya nevah know," a friend used to tease. "Yeah," I sigh. "If only I had known, I never would have . . ." "If only I had recognized the seeds of lust, deception and death I was sowing, I never would have . . ." If only

I had realized that what I do today shapes my future and my children's futures. *If only, if only.*

Is there a direct link from today's choices to tomorrow's realities? Yes! The scriptural principle from Matthew's Gospel clearly states that if the homeowner had kept watch, he would have prevented the theft. The connection is not as easy as, If I cut my finger, I'll bleed. It's more like aging. It sneaks up on me. If I had known what and when and how the "age thief" would come to steal my muscle tone and smooth skin, I would have exercised more and used a better moisturizer when I was young. Or like an extramarital affair, if I had known the legacy of sexual sins left by my affairs, I would never have left my children home alone.

If I, as head of my family after my husband's death, had known at what moment, on what occasion, or in what circumstance the enemy would seduce and sow his seeds of destruction in my family, I would have watched and set up alarm systems and built fences and hired guards. If I had paid attention to the subtle ways he was establishing his stronghold, gaining ground, taking over, usurping authority—if . . . if . . . if. If I had secured the locks, mended the fences, trained the guard dogs, not gone off to a foreign country, I would not have lost sight of the enemy's devices. I would not have suffered the house to be broken up, burglarized, devastated.

I know now one of the times when the thief came. He came when I lied to my children and said, "I'll be gone overnight for a business meeting." "I'll be attending a college reunion with some old friends for the weekend." "I have to work late." I didn't know those were the nights that the thief would break in. I didn't know that my sins would leave the door open for the thief to come and steal my children. If I had known, I would have stayed at home. *Nancy, keep watch.*

*   *   *   *

Our honeymoon suitcases are full of rice and city clothes, matching blue-and-white seersucker suits, white strappy shoes for me, and navy wingtips for Don. Mr. and Mrs. Don Heche drive to Chicago and sign in at the

Brevort Hotel—unleashing our love and laughter. Along with my lacy things and my mother's string of real pearls, I packed a book from the shelves in my father's den—a medical terminology book with awesome pictures of body parts, each page carefully protected by delicate onion-skin. This is one way, the only way for me, to get some sex education. We expose ourselves to the naked drawings and discover what comes next.

We dance at the Palmer House, even when they tell us it's too early in the evening to open the dance floor. Everything is forgiven when we release our embrace and show off our shiny new white-gold wedding bands.

The city holds fewer delights than we expected—we're mostly delighted with each other. We come up for air long enough to see the latest musical, *Oklahoma,* and hurry back to the Brevort.

Groceries are delivered to Heche's Backwater Grocery Store in North Webster on Thursdays, so we need to go home to go to work. Don was an old pro, but I quickly learned how to work the cash register, how to candle eggs, cut the Colby longhorn cheese into very thin slices and fill the candy case. Don's mother cooked beef and noodles and we ate canned vegetables and toasted cheese sandwiches, going back and forth from the kitchen in the back of the house to the front of the store. I had never cooked a meal in my young life, but that didn't seem to be a prerequisite for marriage!

We also went back and forth from the store to Epworth Forest where Don continued his lifeguard duties and I became the secretary to the Executive Administrator of the Warsaw District of the Methodist Church. I was grateful to be relieved of my store duties and received a generous paycheck each week from the Methodist Church. My kind and forgiving boss, Mr. Fenstermacher, even paid me the week I sent out neatly typed letters—quickly and efficiently but without his signature—to all of the ministers in the district.

Before our first married summer was over and we headed back to Bloomington, we were becoming more and more suspicious that I was pregnant. The only thought we had given to this was prompted by my mother's frequent concerned question, "What are you going to do when little Susie comes along?"

Well, we just kept going. We went back to school our sophomore year. Don brought cookies and candy bars to me between classes to try to counteract my nausea. I took a break from classes the second semester and took several correspondence courses. Our friends, Shirley and Elmo, were pregnant again and parked their new 48-foot mobile home right next to our 36-foot one. (Lots of couples do this—we can too.)

"First comes love, then comes marriage, then come Nancy and Don with a baby carriage," so goes the children's rhyme for jumping rope. We thought the baby and carriage would come after college graduation. We had dreamed of a trip to Europe for our graduation present to each other. But after May 5, 1957, we strutted on campus with a baby carriage and a real live baby of our very own. Welcome Susan Claire, named for both grandmothers—"the child that is born on the Sabbath day is bonnie and blithe."

How could we have known that those hot summer nights on the second floor of the administration building at Epworth Forest would be the spawning ground for precious new life—when the bookstore lady, the craft instructor and the director of the weekly Methodist Youth Fellowship camps, each in rooms of their own, lived up there with us?!

Each warm summer night we were reminded, "Be sure to keep your doors open so we can get some good cross ventilation." The 10 x 10-foot rooms each faced the center lounge where visiting pastors sat up way past our bedtime.

*　　*　　*　　*

The TV comedy *Happy Days* is now in re-reruns, ancient history in TV Land. *Leave it to Beaver* is the standard joke to mock the All-American family, mom and apple pie. But I like it. That's what I was planning for life after college. Oh, it's not as if we sat down with our Day-Timer or BlackBerry or financial advisor—we didn't have articulated goals and budgets or spending plans. If we were married, didn't that mean we were the same person? We didn't really have to talk about it—about the details, did we? Didn't the details just fall into place—the money, the career, the house, the white picket fence, vacations, retirement, sex, children, religion? Weren't we supposed to just know? I thought so.

We did want children, of course. We enjoyed church and friends who loved what we loved—Bible studies, prayer meetings, great food, family nights. How could we have known what was going on beneath the surface of these good things? When did it happen? How did it happen? I have to scrape my way through all the bad stuff to get to the edge of any good stuff and wonder if there were really any happy days after all.

I thought I was doing and being exactly what I was meant to do and be. We were with people who loved us, or we found people who loved us in our different churches and neighborhoods. Over a period of years, I learned to bake bread, make applesauce (after Mrs. Tharett, from the church, told me it didn't come only in a jar), sew my children's clothes and can vegetables. What is more satisfying than seeing a beautiful row of canned tomatoes on the scrubbed kitchen counter after a long hot day over the stove?! Or seeing two of my adorable girls fluffing around the room in their pink-and-white-checked ruffled pinafores?

I devoured Scripture with my neighbors while the children napped and the washer and dryer did the dirty work. Another mom, Gerry, whose roomy kitchen we used as a classroom, lugged out the heavy *Strong's Concordance*. Pam, my brilliant neighbor on the other side, opened the *King James Bible* and started reading our selected verses for the day. I wrote the verses in my notebook and recorded the various meanings of the difficult words from the concordance. Then we took each verse and substituted a new word from the concordance for one of the words that puzzled us. We loved getting just a little different twist on the verse as we changed the wording ever so slightly.

I remember those good things. But superimposed over those awesome days of our first season of marriage was a weighty, cumbersome, unyielding force that makes the memories difficult to enjoy today. It was like the medical book that I took on our honeymoon—the onion-skin paper covering the scandalous drawings.

If I stand in the right light, maybe I can see the niceties. If someone reminds me of the fun at Holiday Sands, the summer water playground where we all screamed down the giant slide and balanced on the barrels, maybe I can forget for a moment. But when I lift off the fragile covering, the drawing is garish and harsh. Quick, cover it up! That's enough. I don't want to see it all. Let me stare through the opaque covering as if it's some-body else's story. There is no happy ending.

When one-half of a couple is gone, half of their dream is gone too. I am left with my half of our dream. What good is it? (What good is one shoe? Or one lovebird?) I can't do dinner for one when I learned to prepare it for two. The recipe I have to halve is never quite the same as the original. But this corrupted version is the one remaining—that's all I know for now.

What am I supposed to do? How do I begin again? Start from scratch? No, I'm damaged goods. I'll never be the fresh, young virgin bride again. Did I want to turn the other cheek? Walk the extra mile? Forgive seventy times seven? No, it never entered my mind. I would keep my anger, thank you.

It would be a long time before I would "buck up," before I could recall with fondness the good ol' days, before I got down on my knees and prayed. I wanted to resent the days and weeks and years of sharing meals, sharing children, sharing sex, and then being left with ashes for beauty, mourning for dancing, heaviness for praise.

*   *   *   *

Remember Samson? Talk about an auspicious beginning! Heralded by an angel. Rushed by the Spirit of God. Proclaimed as the deliverer of Israel from their enemy the Philistines. His parents prayed to the Lord and got an answer delivered by a real live angel.

But what I remember about Samson is his silliness and vanity—the disgrace and defeat he leveled on the nation of Israel. He was spoiled and arrogant and demanding—"Get me that woman for my wife," he yelled at his parents. "Why should I explain it to you!" he taunted his wife when she asked for the answer to his riddle.

But the most foolish of all was his humiliation with Delilah, giving in to her seduction and betraying his lifelong Nazirite vow: "Drink no wine or other fermented drink, do not eat anything unclean; no razor may be used on his head, because he is to be set apart to God from birth."[2] When he put his handsome head in her luscious lap and told her everything, he became the victim of her scheming. She called a servant to come and shave off Samson's seven braids of hair. Immediately his strength left him, and the Lord left him also. He was a prophet left powerless. He started out so well—with the honor of being a prophet and judge for the Most High God.

Don and I also started out so well—well loved by all who knew us and passionately in love with each other. Love was butterflies in my stomach when I got within half a mile of his front door. Love was being kissed by a hot-blooded hunk in the dark on the green sofa in my parents' living room. Love was being tangled at the drive-in movies on a summer cloud. We started out so well.

CHAPTER FOUR

Normal

Our new church in Cleveland Heights, Ohio, could have been a foreign land for all its unfamiliar landscape and inhabitants. Don and I—with our two-year-old daughter, Susie, anchored between us—got baptized into fundamentalist Christianity in a friendly rush in the summer of 1959, a true serendipity summer planned by an other-worldly Travel Agent.

We had marked a map of the Cleveland area and targeted all the swimming clubs as possible lifeguard job sites for Don before he began his studies in medical school. We landed a divine appointment at the soon-to-be-renovated Lake Shore Country Club where we met a young couple—Paul and Gerry—whose five children splashed away every sunny day.

Susie made the first introductions. She was enthralled with the attention showered on her by the four beautiful sisters in matching bathing suits. And none of us could resist the charm of their infant baby brother. Day after steamy day, while Don guarded lazy lives around the adult pool, Gerry and I guarded giddy girls around the baby pool and began a life-long, life-changing dialogue. Although I had given my life to religion, I had never surrendered to Jesus. But that's who Gerry talked about. It wasn't about religion; it was about a Person. This definitely required further investigation. "Why don't you visit our church and then come to Sunday dinner with us?" Gerry suggested. We did and we never turned back.

The Methodist Church had never been like this! I was used to seeing people drift idly into church, sit down, routinely read the bulletin, stand, sit, stand again, sing joylessly to the full chords of a pipe organ, recite a prayer, then walk out the door, and only then burst into cheerful chatter.

Now the cheerful chatter was on the inside of the church building. Did everyone know everyone else? It surely seemed that way. And were they carrying their Bibles—to church? I had never taken mine off the bedside table (where I thought Bibles belonged). Where was the pipe organ? And on the wall, instead of a cross, the finance committee had mounted a huge red-and-white thermometer to record the rising level of financial giving for the new building program. It seemed ludicrous—even sacrilegious! But never mind the missing pipe organ and the informality; we were loved, so we became citizens of this new world and learned the language—the do's and don'ts of fundamentalism and its disciples. It wasn't long before we knew everyone else too.

We were courted, romanced and married to this church in a whirlwind love affair. Gerry and Paul were recent converts from Catholicism and had won his brother and her sister, recently married to each other, to the faith as well. Other young couples, seeking friends and faith, joined us in the Builders Sunday School class. Now I knew what abundant life was all about.

It was late-night Bible studies, potluck dinners and babies, babies, babies. It was about developing a relationship with the "Lord," different from the more formal "God" of my religious phase. It was about going to church every time the door opened and going door-to-door when evangelistic fervor exploded in our congregation. It was about taking my Bible off the bedside table and carrying it to church. It was Don in his element, playing the piano for all the ensembles and special musical numbers.

It wasn't just the young couples that became our friends. We were still Prince and Princess, with our pretty little princess, Susie, beside us. We were favorites in the fellowship of these believers. An older couple—"Auntie Merle" and "Uncle Mac" Yost—became Susie's Cleveland grandparents. Their lovely home was lace and linen and highly polished mahogany and elegant ladyfinger delicacies. It was also an African museum. Their daughter and her husband had built a school for missionary children in the Sudan, and Auntie Merle had collected her treasures when she visited her daughter's family there.

*   *   *   *

Our move from Bloomington to Cleveland Heights in May 1959, from being college kids to grown-ups, was a seemingly easy transition. Don had been chosen for a position at Western Reserve Medical School, the prize location for pre-med students around the country that year. I landed a teaching spot in the elementary school a few blocks from our first city apartment and next door to a nursery school that could find room for a two-year-old toddler.

Each smooth day had its routine. It began with Don walking down the hill to med school and Susie and me driving together to our schools. I prayed her through the door into the protective arms of her day-care director, Miss Julie.

This routine ended abruptly six months later when Don came home from the hospital with an announcement: "I've decided to quit med school. I think it's God's will for me to quit—that's all I know. It's the Lord's will."

There was no discussion. (Who can argue with the Lord? Isn't that what this new life is all about anyway?) Now I would have to be content to ponder my lost dream of being a doctor's wife from the perspective of the "Lord's will." It felt like sitting a few rows back in coach with a bag of pretzels while eyeing the first-class passengers who were enjoying filet mignon and a fine red wine. (You can't even use the lavatory in first class!)

Although I might have begun to put two and two together about Don's instability in a career choice, I did not. I quit teaching, took Susie home and waited for him to get a job. "Uncle Mac" made that happen fairly quickly. Then another offer came and someone hired Don as an insurance agent. That was followed by a job in a chemical company, followed by a sales position with the Alexander Hamilton Leadership Correspondence Program. Then he became a top hearing-aid salesman after he conquered embossed matchbook covers and vacation incentive plans. Was this what he meant about God's will when he quit medical school? Susie and I followed him through each open door like well-trained soldiers following their leader, silent and in step.

This new arrangement of Don working and me at home presented us with two opportunities: more babies and more Bible study. So with more time in our schedules, we could dig into Scripture to discover the truths of our cherished faith and we could concentrate on getting pregnant. We did both.

Soon after Susie's fourth birthday, Cynthia Anne Heche was born into our excited, joyful family—joyful for moment. We soon heard Dr. Kennell say, "Something's not quite right. We're having trouble with her breathing. We'll let you know as soon as we know anything."

Then more uncertainties: "We won't want the baby to be breast-fed," the pediatrician announced, breaking my heart as well as a crucial bond between mother and child. "We need to keep track of how much the baby is drinking." So they bound up my life force. They discovered that she had a heart defect and other "troubling" symptoms. Cynthia died within two months.

On the chilly October afternoon of Cynthia's memorial service, "Auntie Merle" gifted me with a promise: "I know the plans I have for you, plans to prosper you and not to harm you, plans to give you a hope and a future."[1] As a young believer, I was unaware that the God of the universe thought about my future, that He purposed to give me hope even through the loss of my infant daughter. But I chose to believe His promise and trust it, even in that moment when this sad event could have stopped me in my tracks. It's not that I can say today, "Oh, *now* I know what God's design was for Cynthia's brief life." I don't know—even these many years later. But God and His Word, and this particular promise, captivated me and continues to be a prominent theme in my life. I don't say this verse as a cliché, as a patronizing pat on the shoulder when trouble comes. I say it as a prayer.

Cynthia was buried in Lakeview Cemetery beside little Donnie Craig, the beloved grandson of Auntie Merle and Uncle Mac, our friends in grief.

*   *   *   *

The study of biblical doctrine held our attention now. In the midst of the chaos of several job changes and the sadness of Cynthia's death, we found a much-needed order and certainty for our lives as we studied the doctrine of Calvinism. We settled into a doctrinal haven of T.U.L.I.P.— Total Depravity, Unconditional Election, Limited Atonement, Irresistible Grace, and Perseverance of the Saints—the five foundations of Calvinism. Every verse we read seemed to confirm the soundness of this doctrine.

The only fly in the theological ointment was the emerging conflict our strict adherence to the doctrine of Calvinism presented to our much-loved Bible-teaching pastor. We tried to convince him of its truth, or rather, some of the men from the Builders Class did. Paul was the self-taught, well-respected teacher of our Sunday School class; Don was the educated scholar, musician, doctor, chemical engineer. Why wouldn't anyone—everyone—believe our passionate presentations, our urgent warnings to turn from "error" to truth?

It was very clear that we had no choice in the matter, not when it came to our faith. We had to follow the truth. We must leave our church and align ourselves with other true believers who valued what we did.

Paul had been communicating with believers in Ashland, Kentucky, who published a weekly newspaper full of Calvinistic doctrine. They were members of the "true church" that traced its beginnings all the way back to John the Baptist. This is what we were looking for. This is what I needed. Stability and predictability. Answers, rules, order for the chaos and uncertainty in my life.

We "divorced" our church and started our own small church. The pastor from Ashland, who wrote and edited the newspaper, came to Cleveland and baptized us in Tiber's swimming pool and "established" us as a true, authentic church descended directly from the line of John the Baptist. We were as close to heaven as we would get for a long time.

The church made its home in our home in Shaker Heights and held services right in our living room. Some of the carpenters in our liberated congregation built, in our basement, a 3 x 3 x 8-foot plywood frame, lined it with huge plastic liners, and christened it the baptistery. (A few years later, when we were showing the house to realtors, we overheard one of them say to her client, "It's kinda creepy—it looks like they have a coffin down here.")

I wanted to do everything as carefully as possible—I wanted to believe the "right" doctrine, be in the "right" church, be baptized by the "right" pastor. If I could make everything look "right," then it would be "right." Right? In retrospect, all of this religiosity served as a brilliant disguise and clever charade for the perversion just beneath the surface. It never occurred to me to pull off the mask. I was part of the act—the straight man (no pun intended) who made the whole thing possible. Ask me no questions, I'll tell you no lies. What did I want to find out anyway?

I was doing my part to set things in order. Each week I had four loaves of gorgeous whole wheat bread—no white sugar, no white flour—cooling on wire racks; the diapers folded just right—corner to corner, edge matching each edge; the peaches—slightly sweetened with natural, unfiltered honey—squared away in the freezer; and the children's toys out of sight where they belonged. Isn't that all I was supposed to do? Don't ask me to try to analyze, scrutinize, probe, pry, suspect, distrust, deduce, infer, think! I'm doing my job—taking care of my children, doing the laundry, sewing, ironing, cleaning. Just let Don do his job!

He was gone so much. I waited for him sometimes, late at night, sitting in the dark, watching for the car headlights to come down Fisher Road and turn into our rutted gravel driveway. If I closed my eyes for a long time and then opened them, would he be home? Or if I took a long, long walk on a sunny afternoon with the children and then came back, would he have a job? If I sang some old hymns—"It is well with my soul"—would God change him and would we be back to "normal?" Or what if he came home and I had to face him while I was angry and hurt and confused? How could I bear to see him face-to-face after all I had conjured in my mind? And what if he never came home? I needed a good country western song to sing my blues! One time I took the car and sat in it all night, away from home and away from him and the children. I wanted him to worry and wonder the way I did when he was late or gone.

I made up in my head all sorts of things he must be doing before he came home in the middle of the night. Funny, he was making up all sorts of things to tell me about what he was doing in the middle of the night. Of course, I was a million miles from the truth, and so was he. Sometimes when he walked through the door, I would scream and cry;

sometimes I tried to be the submissive wife, sympathetic for the hard work and late hours he had to keep. Most of the time I felt helpless and desperate. What could I possibly do to change our circumstances? I kept thinking, *If only he had a full-time job.* I always thought our problems were related to money or lack of it.

*   *   *   *

Nell shares her story with me. She is just like I was years ago—she believes she has her house in order. She certainly has tried hard enough. She volunteers at her church four days a week. She gets home early enough in the afternoon to greet her children when they get off the school bus. She lovingly studies the gold-star chart of chores with each child, counting yesterday's rewards and gently but firmly outlining today's responsibilities. "Let's get going so the house will be nice and clean when Daddy gets home." She starts dinner. "Won't Daddy be happy when he sees everything we've done," she hopes. Hour after disappointing hour they perform. The phone rings. "Oh children, Daddy just called. He said to go ahead and eat without him. He's going to be late tonight," she explains again.

Nell, distracted, fixes plates of dull peas and Kraft macaroni and cheese for herself and the children, asks them about their day, licks the gold stars for the chart and surprises them with an extra one for their good job. Tomorrow she will repeat the ritual. She takes an anti-acid tablet, puts the dishes in the dishwasher and goes to bed, alone. Ask me no questions and I'll tell you no lies.

What will it take for us to turn on the house lights? What will have to happen before we pull open the curtains? How much longer can we wait before we strip off the masks and the costumes to expose the true identity of the actors?

*   *   *   *

The small, tightly knit group of believers became a loving, devoted community of six or seven families. Week by week we rallied together—obedient soldiers marching as to war, zealous for the truth—closer to God and further from the world. I was a perfect candidate for a religious order that required compliant, submissive followers. I had learned— from my childhood upbringing, through my marriage, and now in the church—that silence is golden and quiet submission is expected. This was God's will for me—to be seen and not heard. I didn't get a direct command, but I had heard it clearly in my father's silence and now in my husband's unexplained absences. It made sense for me to function in the same hushed, unquestioning system with our new pastor. "You shouldn't be wearing lipstick, Nancy, or cutting your hair—your hair is your glory," he taught. "It's too much like the world, and we're to be separate from the world. And your slacks are like men's clothing, forbidden in Scripture. Long dresses and loose-fitting smocks and head coverings are more modest. I prefer that all of the women dress like that. And, oh, by the way, the Christmas celebration has its origin in pagan worship and is never mentioned in Scripture. As a church, we won't be celebrating Christmas this year."

Okay.

Don and I bought 40 wooded acres of land outside the city and, along with five other families, built homes in a compound-like setting to keep us out of the world and to keep the world out of us. I didn't read a newspaper or watch television or listen to the radio for nearly 10 years. Don't ask me about Top 40 songs or news events in the late 1960s or early 1970s. I never heard them.

In the meantime, Don and I were praying fervently for another baby. It was four years of waiting 14 days, then the next 14 days, then the next and the next—every monthly cycle was anxiously counted and recount- ed—until the miraculous conception of our third baby. We were full of anxiety and mixed emotions as we drove to MacDonald House hospital in Cleveland for the delivery of our much prayed for "reward from the Lord," as the psalmist sings about our children. Would he or she be healthy? *Please, Lord, let this baby be healthy. That's all we ask.*

A very healthy Nathan Bradlee Heche was born on April 21, 1965, to the happiest couple in the world. Our son was the answer to our prayers. One of our praying friends had promised, "A well-prayed-for baby is a well-blessed baby." The parents are well blessed too.

With each new baby, my role in our marriage and in the church was more clearly defined. Abigail Anne-Maria was born 15 months after Nathan; and Anne Celeste came two and a half years after Abigail. What went on in the outside world held little meaning or significance for me. I was becoming embedded in the life of my family and the other church families. Don was embedded elsewhere. It was hard to pay attention to his comings and goings anyway.

It was easy for me to lose my husband. I was busy nursing babies, sewing little girls' pinafores and playsuits and learning to make spaghetti sauce and veal scaloppini with my Italian neighbors. I had my hands full. Wherever Don was that day or night, we were both doing the Lord's will, weren't we?

One chilly fall afternoon, between naptime and supper time, I heard the car in the driveway. I ran to the door, my usual "Hi, honey," in my next breath. The man who opened the door bore no resemblance to the one who had left earlier that day. It was Don all right, wearing an orange plaid suit and vest and flashy wing-tip shoes. But it was his hair that really alarmed me. It was styled, teased, sprayed and highlighted. Silence served me well that day. What could I say? What was there to say? My "Hi, honey" caught in my throat. I nearly tripped over my long skirt as I backed up to steady myself on the corner of the kitchen table. I dropped Nathan's warm hand and adjusted my head covering over my dull, be-draggled bun. I shifted infant Abigail from one arm to the other and turned to check the roast in the oven. Nathan hid behind my skirt. Abigail was mute.

Why don't I scream and yell and demand some explanation—*Where did you get those clothes? What's going on? Who are you?! Tell me something—anything.* But in seconds, I talk myself into a smile and a reasonable explanation that he is always ahead of his time in style and taste, always the best dressed. *That's what this is,* I thought, *and besides, he needs new clothes for his meetings in town.* And what do I know anyway—I am out of the world and safely sheltered from concerns about fads in fashion. "I think dinner is almost ready," I offer. And everything is back to normal.

CHAPTER FIVE

Dirty Love

I thought it would be the hardest thing I would ever have to do—drive away without even saying good-bye. But the way things were between Gerry and me, we couldn't speak. I felt betrayed by the very woman I loved the most—the one who had led me to the Lord, taught me how to cook, how to love my babies, how to study my Bible—me a young disciple "Timothy" to her mature "apostle Paul."

I had obeyed all the rules that she and her husband, Paul, had imposed on me. Now they had discarded some of them, without any warning, so that their teenage daughters could wear lipstick and mascara. I had forsaken everything for them, for the church—didn't that matter? Couldn't they have called a meeting or mentioned it, even in casual conversation?

And finally an explanation. "We're going to allow our girls to wear makeup as they enter high school," they said out of the blue. "And we'll allow them to wear pants once in awhile. It's a change of our church policy, but we've decided there's no harm in it, for the girls, until they get a little older and come back to following our rules again." What?! Those girls even had to wear split skirts to ride their horses! They were as surprised at this reversal in thinking as I was.

I had been led to believe that my holiness would vanish overnight because of a tube of lipstick and a wand of mascara or a pair of pants. We thought our outward appearance should reflect a commitment to our separation from the world. If Jezebel painted her face, then we would not. If the apostle Peter wrote that there is no wearing of gold jewelry or fine clothes, then we would not. One undotted "i" or one uncrossed "t" and we were in trouble. What did it matter if it's "Pink Passion" lipstick or the antithesis of Calvinism—the heretical Arminian doctrine of free will?! It was all error, and we were to abhor it.

If the head of our church—our pastor and his family—could switch horses in midstream, then either we had the wrong horse or the wrong stream! If this inconsistency were carried to its logical conclusion, we could all be wearing makeup, cutting our hair, wearing pants and removing our head coverings! Unthinkable! In a carefully paced unhitching, disillusioned couple after disillusioned couple began to leave the church.

Many of us still wanted to be a properly established church, so we made a pretense of doing things "right" by having the pastors from Kentucky come to Cleveland and create a branch church from the "mother" church. During that ceremony, the old church members sat silently on one side of the room, staring straight ahead, and the new church members sat silently on the other side doing the same—like partners in a bitter divorce who refuse to speak to or look at one another.

It was the summer of 1971. Don sold our unpainted, uncarpeted, unheated home that we had never finished building and maneuvered our family out of the Amish community of Burton, Ohio, into the sophisticated neighborhood of Cleveland Heights. We must have resembled the Beverly Hillbillies. Actually, we felt more like the children of Israel being delivered out of bondage. We had escaped the harsh and ever-changing, ever-growing burden of a domineering, opportunistic church taskmaster. The passionate lovers had fallen out of love, heartbroken, like fans at a rock concert who discover that the rock star is lip-synching the music.

It took a year to mend my broken heart and survive the culture shock—I cut my waist-length hair in stages, Susie went to ninth grade in long skirts (no pants); and Nathan, Abigail and Anne stayed out of public school. It takes time to meld with city life. The children and I had been sheltered for 12 years in a world where I deferred my decision-making to others. I didn't learn to trust my instincts. If I raised a suspicion or an objection, I was considered ridiculous: "Don't be silly—you don't have any reason to feel like that," Don "comforted" me with his ready charm and easy explanations.

We stayed in Cleveland Heights for a year, where Don flourished as an interior designer in an upscale design studio. Finally, he was in his glory. If he didn't go into a music career, he should be an interior designer. He was marvelous at it—gifted with great taste, loved by his fussy clients, surrounded by extravagance. He even began to make a little money.

He stayed a year and then took a design job in Aurora, Ohio. It required another move, so we packed up and moved into a townhouse close to his work. A year later we bought a "Century" house with its authenticating plaque by the front door, and moved in. This solid 100-year-old house, reliable and trustworthy for more than a century, had roots, stability, immovability. Maybe it was a sign. *Please, Lord, plant us here where we can put down our own roots—raise our children and grandchildren, celebrate birthdays and anniversaries and graduations, grow old together.*

We stayed in Aurora long enough for Susie to graduate from high school in 1975, and to discover a wonderful church for our family. We were evolving into people who wore regular clothes, enjoyed a normal church and had normal friends.

The newly formed church close to Aurora needed someone to direct its music program. There was a prayer group for me, a youth group for Susie, children's programs for the younger children and a ready-made volunteer position for Don as the music director. I took up the challenge of leading a women's neighborhood Bible study. What could be better? I loved it! This was the Promised Land. But all the "milk and honey" in the world couldn't prevent giants from invading the territory. It was shocking and disheartening. The hijinks in the congregation read like some of the sordid stories from the Old Testament.

- The youth pastor, who had accepted his first ministry post, was so involved with the expanding youth program that he neglected his gifted young wife, who stepped out with the chairman of the elder board.
- The second wife of the youth pastor was his children's nanny, who tragically shot herself in her car one winter morning. The troubled nanny had been adopted as an infant by a lonely couple

in the church, but the adoptive mother abandoned her when
the girl was 13.

- The darling of the young wives' group confessed to me 20 years
later that she had been bulimic most of her married life. Her
mother committed suicide when this beauty was 25.

- After breaking up the home of the youth pastor, the same
charming elder had an ongoing affair with the beautiful wife of
the chairman of the building committee. The elder eventually
divorced his wife and children and married the second woman
whose family he had destroyed.

- And oh yes, there was Don's secret—dirty love.

I've often wondered how all the bad stuff could be going on in the
midst of all the good stuff. Maybe rules and rigid leadership keep the Body
of Christ holy and unblemished. For the most part, it seemed to work at
the former church, except for Don, of course.

*   *   *   *

It took a lot of holy intervention to get me to leave our newfound
friends when Don said we were moving to New Jersey for an exciting
new business opportunity. I asked God to convince me that my husband was right, that he had our family's best interest at heart, that this
was one more way to fulfill God's purpose in our lives. All signs pointed to: "Yes. Go. Trust Me." This was the message I heard in every Bible
verse I read, every old hymn I sang. Night and day I asked for assurance,
for reassurance. "Trust Me." I believed this was a step of faith for me.
Besides, Don was traveling to the East Coast a lot and we would be closer to him. "The best is yet to come" was the bait, promised by Don and
inferred from my Bible study.

We moved to Atlantic City, New Jersey, right on the ocean, in February
1977. Don and Neal, an acquaintance from Cleveland, would be leasing
gas and oil rights from landowners in south Jersey for an enterprising New
Yorker. Don's business partner had left his family in Ohio, in order to give

himself wholeheartedly to the new project. Don, in a noble gesture, took his family with him.

It sounded like a great venture, with lots of potential. The East Coast had an elegant ring to it. It seemed as if we were drawn to the ocean as surely as the tide ebbs and flows. The children and I raced to the board-walk—there really is a *board* walk! I shouted my delight to the wind and the waves. Only God could hear me above the glorious roar of His power and splendor in this place. No wonder He brought us here. It's heavenly. We discovered the mighty ocean and the miles of sandy, crab-filled beach. We created our kingdom in the sand, dragging our feet to form the six-foot letters that proclaimed my commitment and my hope: JESUS IS LORD.

We lived in a corporate housing arrangement of sorts—Don's business partner and our family would share a home until we found a suitable one for ourselves. Our expense account bought me carte blanche at the grocery store; so for a limited time, I did the cooking, and we ate like kings.

Some part of the arrangement shifted in about six months when the oil- and gas-leasing scheme went bankrupt. I was worried—more worried than I had ever been. We were a long way from home. Where is the LORD JESUS?

Not to worry. Neal, ever the engaging business partner, had another opportunity in New York. His engineer friend had a hot item to sell to electric companies to revolutionize the way electric meters were read. *Oh, good.* I felt relieved and confident that Don would figure it out one more time. (Call me crazy.)

I still can't put two and two together. There are extended trips to New York to discuss the new business. It's a mystery to me, but Don is so smart that he can surely make it happen this time. *Of course, honey, I understand, you have late meetings. Of course you have to be gone this weekend. Of course, honey, we'll be fine.* How many moves, how many trips, how many off-the-wall excuses, how many prickly little illnesses would it take? Not too many more. We were getting close to our final hour.

The rent was six months past due. We had received several warnings from our landlord. I wondered, *How far will his goodwill reach? How long will we dangle on this brink of grace?* I stood at the counter in the kitchen of our (his) beach house, looking out to the ocean, our front yard, and murmured, "Things will never be the same."

Surely there's a deal ripe and ready to fall into our hands so that we can taste the life of luxury that Don has always fancied for us. He picks me up from my new job at the brokerage firm in Atlantic City. We ride together now, in our bank-owned Cadillac, counting our unhatched chickens as we wait in line to cross the familiar Ocean City Bridge. It's just a matter of time until our ship comes in, isn't it?

*   *   *   *

When did the lightbulb go on? What was the grand epiphany, the aha! that set me off on a job search? Desperation, fear and anxiety. My husband was not yet providing for us. *I guess it's up to me.* My father used to say, "Get an education. Be a teacher, so you can get a job if anything happens." Maybe his prophecy was being fulfilled. Please understand that the lightbulb, the epiphany, the aha! had nothing to do with some brilliant deduction on my part that there was something going on with Don besides the job issue. I am still clueless, even though our finances are a disaster. Food came from heaven, I guess. I have no recollection how or where money appeared. We had sold our wonderful house on Ventnor Avenue of Monopoly fame. Don had used the money, for what I didn't have a clue. (It's not as much of a mystery to me now as it used to be.) We never talked about money except for me to beg, "Please, just get a steady job so we can pay the bills." His reply was, "This deal will probably close by next Tuesday and my share is about one billion dollars!" No kidding. Billion. Capital B. That's what he said over and over. And that's what I believed, over and over.

*   *   *   *

"Wait till you hear this!" I sing into the telephone. "I came across this amazing description of Don and me in one of my graduate school textbooks. I could hardly believe it!" My daughter Anne is listening on the phone in L.A. Steve Martin, her current boyfriend, is standing by. He will translate for me.

"What does 'Folie à Deux' mean?" I ask.

"A foolish thing for two," Steve says. "What's up?"

I get the information I need. "A foolish thing for two . . ." I read to them the text-book description over the phone:

297.3 Shared Psychotic Disorder, *"Folie à Deux."* Diagnostic Features: The essential feature of Shared Psychotic Disorder is a delusion that develops in an individual [Nancy] who is involved in a close relationship with another person [Don] . . . who already has a Psychotic Disorder with prominent delusions.

The individual [Nancy] comes to share the delusional beliefs of the primary case [Don] in whole or in part . . . [e.g., that the primary case—Don—will soon receive a business contract for $2 million, allowing the family to purchase a much larger home with a swimming pool].

Usually the primary case in Shared Psychotic Disorder is dominant in the relationship and gradually imposes the delusional system on the more passive and initially healthy second person.

Individuals who come to share delusional beliefs are often related by blood or marriage and have lived together for a long time [in our case, 25 years], sometimes in relative social isolation [our commune-like church experience].

If the relationship with the primary case is interrupted, [Don dies] the delusional beliefs of the other individual usually diminish or disappear. Individuals with this disorder rarely seek treatment. Limited evidence suggests that Shared Psychotic Disorder is somewhat more common in women than in men. (*Diagnostic and Statistical Manual of Mental Disorders, IV*, 1994, p. 305.)

This description is a scientific classification of my marriage, taken from the diagnostic handbook used by physicians, psychologists and psychiatrists. How did they know us so well?! Get this: *We* seriously looked at buying a mansion while we were homeless. Although we were flat broke, living with our generous friends, we actually toured a million-dollar estate outside Manhattan with a real estate broker and spoke to her as if we could manage the asking price in the very near future. The maid and gardener would stay, Don recommended. We even enrolled our children in a private academy in New York, and signed papers on the basis of the imminent closing on a billion-dollar deal. *Folie à Deux.*

*   *   *   *

As we turn into the driveway, we see our children stranded on the front steps, unable to get into the house. My heart sinks. Don calls out to them, "Hey, kids, what's going on?" He can act so innocent. It is October 4, 1981.

"There's a sign on the door," they say in an accusing tone, well aware of our elusive fortune and shaky reputation. "It says the sheriff has been here and we're locked out."

I think I might throw up. What kind of razzle-dazzle will Don say to explain this? This was probably the first shattering dose of reality that would alert us to our long road of destruction and devastation.

Our embarrassed children, 13, 16 and 17, bombard us with questions. Where are we going to do our homework? How will I get my clothes, toothbrush or makeup? Where are we going to sleep? What are we going to tell our friends? What about dinner?

This is not our first encounter with the law. In Shaker Heights, officers came to our door several times to say that our electricity would be turned off in 24 hours; in Burton we were told our mortgage would be foreclosed; another time I was told that my husband was "kiting" checks, whatever in the world that meant; in Aurora our car was repossessed; in Ventnor our mortgage *was* foreclosed. Oh yes, we were well acquainted with the anxiety and shame that accompanies a visit by the law.

I am just about at my wit's end. How many more phone calls before the long-awaited much-negotiated call that says the deal has *actually* closed, the money is *actually* in the bank? How long before the congratulations—we've *actually* done it? Do I really believe Don? Yes. But I'm getting pretty discouraged. If we haven't hit bottom yet, what will it take?

We are evicted from our home, repossessed of our Cadillac, now riding only on my $800-a-month paycheck from Prudential Bache Securities. We collapse into the charitable arms of loving friends from our church in Ocean City. Their handsome sons are the same ages as Nathan and Abigail. Their older daughter will serve as a substitute big sister while Susan is living in New York. They give up their bedrooms to make room for our displaced family of five.

*   *   *   *

Was this all a blunder on my part? Were the 25 years of marriage to a man who lived a secret life and ultimately betrayed me and our children and lots of other unsuspecting people, and died of AIDS, all just a miscalculation? I don't think so. I loved him. I loved him at 16 and 19 and 44. Do I wish for a clean sweep, like my computer hard drive needs, to get rid of the virus? "We have to erase everything," the computer geek tells me over the phone. Would I really like to erase everything?

What I regret—no, it's not regret, it's grief. What I grieve is the loss of a husband who is 65 *with* me, a father for my daughters, a grandfather for my grandchildren. It's the loss of some "American dream" that I dreamed in high school and college and early married life. It's both loss and reality. Life is difficult. But I wouldn't have married someone else, so it's foolish for me to wonder what it would have been like if I had. "Acknowledge it, Nancy, not 'buck up,' but acknowledge it, mourn it, find the giftedness in it," my therapist, Bob Sears, said to me. Find the giftedness in it? I'm not ready for that.

*   *   *   *

This new adopted home with friends has all the heart we need. The problem is that the damage is done. No amount of warmth and support can save us now from the rapid spin and seduction of other affections. The secrecy of my husband's sexual sin did not prevent illicit lust from invading our home. We all picked it up—osmosis? evil spirits? Whatever. We got it. My children and I fall into the arms of less charitable lovers.

In January 1982, four months after we moved in with friends, at the request of our host, Don moved to New York to get his act together. In February, the children and I moved into our first apartment. I stood with my friend Jan in the tiny second-floor apartment over the real estate office in Ocean City and cried with shock and realization. I alone am responsible for paying the rent on what we now call home and what one friend later called a hovel. Every month I will write a check that won't bounce to the owner of the blue-and-white shuttered office downstairs.

Almost every evening my three disoriented teenage children sit with me in the 5 x 5-foot back porch that serves as a dining room. We add up our expenses in one column and our income in another. We all work several jobs to ensure that there is more income than outgo. Anne babysits for friends and performs at the local dinner theater (she gets fed there and doesn't have to worry about her next meal); Abigail cleans the business office downstairs, much to her chagrin, and works at the fruit stand on Ocean Avenue where she regularly steals money to send to Don in New York. She parades as a beach-chair girl in the summer. Nathan shovels the random snow and bags groceries at my favorite A & P. I think the manager liked me, so it was an easy interview for Nathan.

*   *   *   *

Now the delusional beliefs are diminishing, just as the diagnostic textbook predicted. My relationship with the "primary case" is interrupted. Don is in New York—gone. In walk "Tom" and "Dick" and "Harry," and . . . and . . . other names and faces that I wish I could forget. All it took was one look, and then the next, for me to get lost. I didn't really see it as lost at the time. It was more like getting adjusted—suddenly a new job, a new world, new exemptions. Overnight my world of teenagers and meal planning and homemaking and church and neighborhood Bible studies was turned into the world of stocks and bonds and debauchery.

I didn't know what was missing for me emotionally in my marriage, but when I was seen, and then seen again, I easily opened myself to receive it without having to name it. Nothing had prepared me for this. I had been so shocked at the stories of the affairs at the church. How could Christians do that! And now, here I was, still Nancy, (*still me, Lord*), still a Christian, but I just couldn't make it without this man, this attention, this touch.

Before long I was so caught up in the ways of this new world that I wondered if people were getting "saved" any longer. I could totally justify my flirtations and fornications because everyone I knew was doing the same thing. Who *didn't* do it? Every voice I heard drew me closer. "This is our song," I heard "Dick" say over the phone. "Listen to Willie Nelson, 'You were always on my mind, you were always on my mind.'" No one ever said that to me. *Say it again.*

I began to imagine what it would be like to be married to someone with money, to someone who would long to be with me, crave my touch, buy me things. I could live in luxury—what a break! When wealthy "Tom" casually spoke about the future one night, he added that he wouldn't marry me, even if he divorced his faithful snooty wife. *What?! What was this all about if it wasn't about preparation for marriage?* And "Dick" said, "Well, I never cheated on my wife before. I really just see you as a kind of insurance policy at these business meetings." *Are you kidding! What do you mean? I had myself married and moved out to your ranch.* Don was on one side of dirty love; am I on the other side? I can't stand it and I can't let it go.

I left a land of bondage many years ago and here I am in another kind of bondage that is breaking my heart again. Maybe this is a delusion of my own making. Surely one of these men will love me enough to leave everything, everyone, for me. "Oh, Nancy, I'll never get a divorce because of my children." *Oh.* But even then, with no intention of getting anything more, ever, I still can't say it to him—I can't say: "Well, then, I never want to see you again." I asked "Harry" if he loved me. He just grinned. "You're so needy you don't even know what love is." Well, whatever this is, I need it, whatever he wants to call it.

I tried to talk about my faith, my Bible, my other life. I tried to choose it, but I didn't. It wasn't as if I shook my fist at God and said, "I'm going to stop reading my Bible and praying to You, and I'm going to start sinning the best way I know how." Or, "Today when 'Tom' comes into the office, I'm going to ask him to let me spend the night with him at the casino on the boardwalk." Or, "Tonight I'll lie to my children about a business meeting and stay out all night." No, I just put a few things in my briefcase, walked to his waiting Jaguar when the office closed, and began a seven-year, on-again off-again affair with a man who would never rescue me, never save me.

Now I know why the brilliant youth pastor's wife was an easy mark for the church elder. She had the same pain, the same choices I had. But she couldn't resist any more than I could. Did the devil make us do it? Could Jesus have stopped us? Why wasn't our faith, our commitment, our teaching and preaching and training, our love for the Word and the Lord enough to keep us pure? I'm not sure. I only know that now, years later, I am able to make different choices.

I wrestled with the accepted wisdom that God is punishing me, that I have brought these calamities on myself—ruining my life *and* my children's lives.

On the other hand, I believe that Jesus, on that excruciating cross, took the punishment for all my sins—past, present, future. This is "discipline," the softer word for the pain I suffer at God's sovereign Hand. This proves that God loves me because He "disciplines" me, someone says. It is excruciating love. Will I live through it? If I confess my sin and repent and break off the illicit affairs, will You make everything all better? Will I ever be good enough, obedient enough, holy, righteous, sanctified, justified, redeemed enough?

Today when one of my counseling clients talks about her/his affair, I get it. I used to shake my finger, wag my tongue, scold, attack. That was before I did the same thing. I understand them a little bit more now. I understand some of the hurt that left me, and them, so vulnerable.

Please know that I'm so sorry I left a legacy of sexual sin for my children. I deeply regret the decisions I made many years ago. But my brokenness today helps me know that sometimes there are reasons for doing what we do. It all makes sense when we listen to someone's story, when we tell our story—when the truth comes out. I don't encourage unhealthy behavior, but I can see that what was done made sense in the moment, in the pain, in the hurt, in the anger, fear, and loss, in the loneliness. Sometimes the experience of hearing someone with a compassionate heart say, "I'm sorry. You must have had a really difficult time," brings relief and comfort that begins the healing process. It sounds good to me. It's the gentle invitation to The Way, The Truth and The Life.

"Don't ask questions"—our family never talked about anything. The Prickett family, Washington D.C., 1945. Nancy (left) with parents (Susan and Richard) and sister, Penny

Sisters, Sisters. Three-year-old identical twins, Nancy (left) and Penny, 1940.

"Tea for Two, 1996," Nancy and Penny

It started out so well. Don and Nancy, 19 years old, married June 10, 1956

The perfect family, 1970. Nancy and Don with their children (left to right) Susan, 13, Nathan, 5, Abigail, 3 1/2, Anne, 1.

1980—three years before ground zero. Don and Nancy, with the three youngest children, Abigail 13 1/2, Nathan, 15, Anne, 11 (left to right). Susan is married now.

The Heche women.
Abigail and Anne, 1991

Anne and Nancy at the Telluride Film
Festival in Colorado, 1995

Abigail, Anne (wearing cap) and
Nancy during the filming of Volcano,
October 1996.

Summer 2005. Nancy and Abigail (far left) surrounded by the Bergmans, Nancy's eldest daughter's family. (left to right) Elise, Jud & Susan, Natalie, Ben. Only Elliot, the oldest grandchild, not pictured. He was traveling with his band Nomo.

Dr. Nancy. Graduation day at Garrett Evangelical Theological Seminary, Evanston, Illinois, 2003

Christmas Eve 2002. Nancy with her daughter Abigail, and grandchildren: (top to bottom) Elliot, Elise, Ben, Natalie

CHAPTER SIX

Darkness

"Mom, get the *New York Times* Sunday magazine section and read the article on page 3." It is Susan's voice on the phone, calling from her Yonkers apartment. She and her husband, Jud, are living there while Jud completes the MBA program at Columbia University in New York City. It is February 6, 1983. Don is lying in the hospital suffering from a number of mysterious ailments. "This article describes all of the stuff that Dad has been complaining about for the last year or so," she says with a frantic note in her voice. "Swollen glands, fatigue, weight loss, pneumonia, skin eruptions."

I get in the car and drive to the nearest newsstand—across the bridge to Margate, because all the shops close down in Ocean City on Sundays. I read, "Medicine's brightest and best have not yet solved the puzzle of Acquired Immune Deficiency Syndrome . . . a grab-bag of rare but ravaging diseases. The disease has hit homosexual men, users of intravenous drugs, Haitians, and hemophiliacs." *Hmmmm, he's not Haitian, and he's not a hemophiliac. I don't know about drugs, but it seems to narrow down the choice to homosexual men.* I don't believe it—I can't believe it.

"Everything about AIDS looks as though it is contagious," the story continues. I want to scream. I can't talk to anyone about this. How do I grasp this horrible allegation? Am I going to get it too? This can't be happening.

The next day, I rush to catch a bus to New York, hunt my way to Bellevue Hospital and scream at a ghost of a man, incoherent now, hairpiece askew. He offers a few pitiful words in response to my tirade. "It's not me . . . it's the people I work with in the design business."

Even on his deathbed he's a liar. His usual shell-game antic—it looks like this, but it's really this—shifting blame, defending himself to himself, shifting himself right into an honest grave.

"WHAT IS GOING ON? WHAT *HAS* BEEN GOING ON?" I demand, to the air. I will see him one more time before he dies.

A week later, three weeks before Don dies, there is an article in *Science* magazine (February 10, 1983) describing a research project that uncovers the one common element among a hundred known cases of AIDS patients: the use of amyl nitrites. The magazine article says that these are "stimulants, volatile liquids sniffed from ampoules or little bottles, most often called poppers with names such as *Locker Room* or *Rush,* and used almost exclusively by gays."

What? Don and I had used the "poppers" together. When we first moved to Atlantic City and were living in the house with Don's "business" partner, we were given some little bottles of the dizzying stuff "to enhance our sex life."

"Good, huh?" Neal, the generous donor said, and applauded with a giggle. As I read this article, the pieces were coming together. So Neal was also a homosexual. I had never guessed. Why would I? What was this business deal really?

But I'm a very non-gay wife coaxed into sniffing the poppers as a novelty for *our* sex life. It seemed innocent enough. Why would I question him? What was there to find out? The unexpected information in the magazine story was another deadly sign pointing directly to Don's homosexual activity. I am still trying to make sense of his past, of our past. This paragraph about the poppers was a devastating clue.

The article went on to say that the 100 AIDS patients with the common link of using amyl nitrites often had a history of sexually transmitted diseases such as *hepatitis.* Another piece of the puzzle. When we lived in Aurora, when Don met Neal, Don got very sick and was diagnosed with hepatitis. His skin and the whites of his eyes were a sickening yellow clue to the liver damage that accompanies the disease. I spent dutiful hours reading to him as he lay swathed on the shaded living-room sofa while the children lived in a hush all that year. I reserved a corner of the gold-speckled Formica kitchen counter for his sterilized glass and fork and spoon. He blamed the illness on some bad seafood. We accepted the explanation—it happens.

But the truth comes out in one short sentence from the doctor at Bellevue Hospital.

✳   ✳   ✳   ✳

The last week of February 1983, Abigail and I go to New York. Our plan was to go to the hospital on Friday night and then stay overnight with Susan and Jud and our darling 18-month-old Elliot. I was scheduled to take the Series Seven exam for my brokerage license all day on Saturday.

In the hospital consulting room, the young doctor met with Abigail and me and said, "Hasn't anyone told you, Mrs. Heche? Your husband is dying of AIDS." I didn't see Don that night. I didn't want to see him ever again. He would die of AIDS in three weeks.

We went to Susan's and broke the news. I took the exam the next day, and Abigail and I went back to Ocean City. Nathan and Anne listen to us describe the scene in the hospital. "He has AIDS," I said. "He's probably a homosexual." I am stoic, calm, silent. I have nothing more to say, or to give.

"I'm not surprised," Anne says, home for the afternoon after her performance at the dinner theater. "I've seen some there." She tells us now about observing Don's unusual behavior—applying bronzer and mascara, primping with a new hairpiece, resting most of the day, evidently jobless—when he spent a few weeks with the children in Ocean City while I was in Indiana having a hysterectomy. Not surprised? Anne is more aware than I am. She had evidently been putting some pieces of the puzzle together one oddity at a time.

Me? I forced myself to search our unstable marital history for other matching, or mismatching, pieces or people. Let's see. There were two quirky women, smiling and doting on our children, who sold Don (for a nonsufficient-funds check of $6,000) 57 large oil paintings and several charcoal and pastel drawings. He was doing the interior design work in their newly purchased home in Aurora. They had acquired the paintings from the estate of Glenn Cooper Henshaw, a not-so-well-known artist in Nashville, Indiana. They expected to cash in on their investment when the painter became better known or when Don vended them to his design clients, whichever came first. B. and L., the friendly women, had one king-size bed in their house. It struck me as kind of crowded. *They must not have furnished the second bedroom yet,* I thought at the time.

"The rest of their furniture hasn't arrived," Don explained smoothly. The women included Don in numerous business affairs—it seemed like a good business connection.

Eight or ten years after Don died, and Susan was writing her book about our family, she asked me if I could find B. and L. for her. She wanted to see if they could shed any light on Don's secret life. Could they confirm our suspicions? I made one phone call to a number in my old address book. L. answered the phone, and I reacquainted myself, telling her that Don had died. Her first question was, "Did he die of AIDS?" The very first question. I was not prepared for such immediate evidence of their collusion with Don to keep his double life a secret. "They not only continue to do these very things but also approve of those who practice them," wrote the apostle Paul in the book of Romans, when he was naming some of the practices of those who "suppress the truth."

L. later said to Susan, "Don didn't hurt anyone but himself." She told Susan that what he did was his business and we had no right to question him; it was all behind closed doors. (Didn't hurt anyone but himself? Behind closed doors? Please.) How could she not have any idea of the hurt his family was suffering? And how had they survived the AIDS epidemic? I guess they were smarter than Don, Mr. Phi Beta Kappa. What good did all his brains do him, or me? Or any of us?

And there was another piece of the puzzle: There was a handsome older man whom I will call B. V. He was a little too charming, sort of oily, and walked with his pelvis thrust out, sort of sashaying himself forward. He was married, with seven children, I think. He schmoozed Don into the insurance business when we were seniors in college. Their strategy was that Don would make appointments with other pre-med students, soon-to-be-rich young doctors who could afford a nice chunk of life insurance, and B. V. would come to the campus on Saturdays to meet his prospects.

Don and B. V. spent each Saturday together—all day—working, and meeting prospects? I didn't question it. But could Don *really* get that many med students to take an hour or more on a Saturday study day at the lab to listen to B. V. talk about insurance? The two salesmen would come back to our college home for dinner—a 36-foot long, 8-foot wide mobile home. The arrangement worked for me, and it would pay off at graduation when B. V. handed Don a check for $3,000. What a nice guy! But why was he so generous to us?

Other clues? Oh, yes. Now I can see them. Don and I were taking a train to Ft. Wayne from Wheaton, where Susan had her senior art exhibition, preparing for her graduation. Don found a sleeper coach for us for the midnight trip. I settled in and he went to get "something." He didn't return until dawn, saying that he had met "the most interesting guy" on the way to the men's room.

Another time he sat up all night with one of the musicians from a group that entertained our local church on Sunday evening. "The guy made some advances toward me," Don said, making it sound so shocking when he mentioned it to me later. Yes, I agreed, it is shocking.

There were other men. The pastor of one of the largest churches in Ocean City met me on the street one day and commented, out of the blue, "Your husband is a very complicated man." What in the world did he mean? How did he even know Don? The soloist of the fashionable church a few blocks from the beach—who seemed to need a lot of extra rehearsal time; a visiting prophetic teacher who sought Don out after the conference, or vice versa. Don't even let me think of all the places they desecrated. And how did they know the other was "interested," or available? Talk about an effective secret "underground" system!

Earlier memories with old red flags:

Don rehearses with the well-loved baritone soloist for the couples' conference at Sawmill Creek Conference Center on Lake Erie. "We'll be working late," Don says to my parents and me—we're all guests at the conference. "Why don't you go back to the room and I'll see you later." Much later.

"The men I meet in New York say that I'm one of the most handsome men they know." (What husband tells his wife something like that?)

"One of the guys at the 'Y' made a pass at me when we were in the shower after our basketball game."

"While I'm in New York, I'm going meet some very successful men who will help me once and for all get these deals consummated. I won't be home this weekend. We're going to Montauk for a business meeting. Pray for us."

"These gifts of food and clothes—steaks, luscious fresh fruit, a sweet mink jacket—are from one of my wealthy friends in New York. He knows how much I love my family and that we're a little tight on money right now."

"E. gave me this small packet of powdery stuff—he thinks our sex life needs some pizzazz!"

"That's not my stuff in my bag—I'm carrying it for someone else."

"I'm taking a part-time job at a short-order joint just to get some cash. It's down in that section called 'Boy's Town,' kind of a hangout for homosexual men. But it's the quickest cash I can get."

"It's so late, honey, and I'm really tired. Let's wait till I'm up for it."

"Oh, it's so late, honey, and I'm really tired. Let's wait till I'm up for it."

"Oh, sorry. It's so late, and I'm really tired. Let's wait till I'm up for it."

"It's so late, honey, and I'm really tired. Let's wait till I'm up for it."

*   *   *   *

On Saturday morning, March 5, 1983, Abigail came into my bedroom to tell me Don died the night before. Abigail had come home from cheerleading practice and was the only one to get the phone call. We sat in bed and cried together. *What do we do now?*

The people at The Lamb's Church, where Don had been attending—a gentle, loving Nazarene congregation near Times Square in New York—called us on Sunday morning and invited us to a memorial service for him that evening. I felt obligated to join them—I wasn't doing anything for him myself. Some friends drove us to New York. We got a glimpse into Don's final faith community. They believed that he had recommitted his life to the Lord. *Good for him.*

The pastor had burned all of Don's clothes, including a new navy cashmere coat, because he didn't know at the time how the AIDS virus was passed. Don could afford a cashmere coat when the children and I had about eight jobs among us so that we could pay the rent. (Or maybe it was a gift to him from one of his thousand fellow prisoners.)

I will never say the word "homosexual." I will tell people—if anyone asks—that Don died of cancer. *I don't have to tell the awful truth, do I? It's all the same lie, the same betrayal and deception now anyway, isn't it? What he professed and what he actually lived?* Recover from the lie and you must then heal from the truth. What difference did it make how he died? "He died one stranger at a time until he finally caught it and could pass it along," my daughter Susan wrote in her 1994 memoir *Anonymity*.

The girls reflect on the consequences of living with a dreamer, with a liar. It produces a haunting fever: What is true? What is false? "We were kept busy filling the many chambers of his dreams, his delusions," Susan wrote. His grandiosity, his fear, his pretense keeps them hovering between arrogance and unworthiness. They wonder, *Why wouldn't everyone love me?!* and *Who will ever love me?*

"What is true? If I can't believe my father, who *can* I believe? On the other hand, why is it that I think I don't believe him? When are the dreams that could revive my waning confidence going to come true?"

"Isn't a child entitled to be fathered by a man who loves women, if not one's mother, for life?" Susan asks one unanswered question after another.

She reminisces, "I still love him. He was my first love—the one who floated me onto his shoulders so that I could almost reach the shooting star. No way to give him another chance, to try harder, . . . so other men become substitutes. They play along for awhile, attached to our devotion."

Anne shudders. "Every time I start getting close to a man physically, I cringe to think: *Oh, now I'm feeling toward him the way Dad would have.* That shuts me right down."

Wife and children have to keep up his con. It started out so well. People are watching for the trumpeted successes. We will wring survival out of every rag of hope. We discover the huge betrayal and the indescribable loss of lives endured with a bisexual husband and a homosexual father.

*   *   *   *

When Don died, I was cast off by the church I attended. Or maybe I did the casting off? Whatever. No one came to see me. Our friends from the church where Don had directed the choir and played the organ and showcased our children did not know what to do, I guess. Their whole world was built around husbands and wives. What do you do with a single mother whose husband has disappeared mysteriously and died mysteriously? You can be nice to the children, but what to do with the wife? I couldn't remember anyone saying to me, "I'm so sorry your husband died." But I can't blame them. I hardly mourned him myself.

It was the same for Neil's angry wife. I talked to her a few years ago, just out of curiosity. She said, "I gave him the best years of my life. Who wants me now? I'm damaged goods. And then he dies of AIDS and leaves me, leaves us—three children—to figure it out for ourselves. I despise him."

*   *   *   *

Don's death took us to the depths of despair. It was the savage, sickening end of our beautiful, perfect Christian family. What could be worse? But nothing could have prepared us for what was to come—the next tragedy, the unfathomable pain and heartache.

Whatever grieving was missing when Don died was reconciled by inconsolable sorrow when Nathan died three months later in a car accident. It was 6:00 a.m., on June 4, 1983. He drove into a tree and died instantly. He was scheduled to take his S.A.T.s that Saturday morning, one week before his high school graduation.

I was in New York that Saturday morning, filled with enormous hope, fascinating a guy who, in my mind, was meant to be a suitable husband for me. The weekend was staged by my married lover, who was not ever going to be free to be my husband. My New York suitor was designing a rendezvous meant to woo, win and bed me all in one fast weekend. I, on the other hand, was imagining an honest romance this time, a sex-free soirée where we would get to know each other in a slow, warm intimacy.

Nathan had driven me to the bus station in Ocean City late Friday afternoon. It would be the last time I would ever see him. For that weekend he would own our sub-compact car, the only car we could afford, purchased from the car dealership of one of my rich married lovers. What price my frugality, my lover's indifference? His secrecy? He had three or four sons of his own—he could have known better than to sell a tin car to a family with a teenage son. The car probably cost me Nathan's life.

Nathan broke my heart with every tease, with every shine. My only son, born to blessing, held my highest hope for happiness. Tall, light, handsome, popular and bright, he was his sisters' antagonist and his friends' hero. He played tennis, ran track and fell in love with Vanessa, an Italian beauty with dark curls and passionate eyes.

Early Saturday morning, in a stranger's New York garden apartment, I got a phone call. A New Jersey state trooper was on the line. "Your son has been involved in a fatal accident," he said. My first thought was, *He's telling me that Nathan was in an accident where someone else was killed.* My next thought was, *Oh, no, you mean Nathan.* After that I only remember the two-and-a-half-hour drive from Manhattan to Ocean City in the old Cadillac convertible, drowning in silence with a stranger wearing a soft, sage-green jacket who had been thrown into our tragic drama.

Abigail had been routed from her boyfriend's bed to identify Nathan's body. Anne was gathered from her friend's house. I reached Susan by phone in Chicago. From somewhere far away I was reminded that sometime in the very distant future I would know that God works all things together for my good to make me more like Jesus. I had been teaching the Bible to young women for several years, and that was the one verse I knew today.

Hundreds of kids lined up around the church for the service three days later. The high school choir sang "Up Where We Belong." Nathan's voice and acting coach sang from the musical *Pippin.* It seemed just right at the time.

I've gotta be where my spirit can be free,
Got to find my corner of the sky.

After the service, the grieving women from the church prepared casseroles and salads and desserts at our mournful second-floor apartment. They rearranged all of the furniture to make room for everyone who wanted to share their love for Nathan. I remember walking into the chaos and confusion and telling them to put the furniture back where it belonged. I'd had enough chaos for one day.

Why would I go on living? I can't stand to be alive with Nathan dead. I might as well be dead myself. I wish I were dead. This didn't really happen, not to Nathan. When Don died, I was relieved—*Now we can get on with our lives,* I thought. But this. No. Never. Never, never, never. I will not give up my son. *Don't you remember—he was the miracle child born to us after baby Cynthia died. Nathan was much prayed for, much blessed. This cannot be the end of Nathan, gift of God. Who's next? What's next?*

For days I lay in the middle of the floor and screamed and cried. Don't talk to me, don't touch me, don't feed me. And please, *please* don't give me a Bible verse. I know them all. They don't work right now. I will never be able to get off the floor, leave my apartment, go to work, cook a meal or smile again. I have lost my son, my only son. I cut his wonderful hair just last week. I washed and folded his clothes. We talked about Vanessa, his forever girlfriend. I can't even look in his closet or dresser now. Nathan will be back. I *need* him.

To this day, I cannot take it in. Please believe me, you who did not know him; I did have a son, the only brother to my four daughters.

✳   ✳   ✳   ✳

Last summer, I answered the phone to a stranger's voice. "Hi, Nancy, this is Jeff Winter." He introduced himself as Nathan's youth pastor in Ocean City during the last few weeks of Nathan's life. Then he went on to say that one of his colleagues whom I had met at the Exodus International conference in North Carolina a few weeks prior, mentioned my name to him as a possible speaker for his 2006 summer conference with the Presbyterian Church USA. He immediately made the family connection. He told me on the phone, "Nathan came to my home on Sunday nights for youth group. I remember his warm personality, such a neat young man. I want you to know that he was truly committed to Jesus Christ. I don't know if it was a new commitment or a recommitment, but he loved Jesus."

I cried as he described the exuberant young disciple who is the light of my life.

*   *   *   *

I wish I could tell you that these two tragedies—my husband's death from AIDS and my son's death in a car accident—shook the holy fear of God into my heart and set my feet on the straight and narrow path. Well, they did, for about a month. I told my lover that I absolutely could not see him, would not be with him. But I needed him. I needed a flesh-and-blood savior. I needed anything and everything he would give me. I could hardly stand up without him. He would help me "put one foot in front of the other and try to get through each day," like Tom Hanks said in the film *Sleepless in Seattle*. I finally did get up, stand up, go to work and carry on my weekly affair with my familiar lover almost as if nothing had happened. My girls and I had no counseling, no spiritual support and didn't know where to find it.

*   *   *   *

Within two months, we moved to Chicago—my daughters Abigail and Anne and I. We are survivors. "We are the people who live," says Ma Joad in *Grapes of Wrath*. I passed my brokerage license exam and would work as a stockbroker in the Chicago office of Prudential Bache Securities. Susan and Jud and Elliot were already here. Abigail had been accepted at Wheaton College—she and Nathan had enrolled together as freshmen at the Christian liberal arts college outside Chicago. My sister and her family were close by in Indiana, along with my mother. It was the logical thing to do—such a safe plan, a cozy healing family a short drive away and the spiritual haven of Wheaton for Abigail an hour's train ride away. I had paid my dues to the East coast. "You need to get out of here," my mister said. "You'll have another life somewhere else. This is not the end of the world." *Easy for you to say.*

Our lives were a mess. I couldn't break the emotional ties with my lover even though I had moved 500 miles away. I found a few other admirers in Chicago whom I chose to try to patch up my broken heart. I kept excusing my sin by saying I just can't stop this yet. I am needed; I deserve some care. I just can't . . . yet. It hurt just to think of the void I would feel if I left.

Abigail got kicked out of Wheaton for sleeping with her football-playing boyfriend and moved to the city where she tried to satisfy her father hunger in the dark worlds of drugs, exotic dancing and prostitution. "If Dad can live recklessly, so can I," she boasted out of one side of her well-painted mouth. "Will anyone ever love me enough? Will anyone ever give me what my father never did, and never will?" she sobbed out of the other. She said she was afraid she didn't want to get better. "I feel useless—why am I even here? The only reason I stay is you, Mom."

Anne describes one of her therapy sessions when she was living in New York in which she has a temper tantrum, expressing her merciless anger that Don was never coming back. "Daddy . . . simply . . . isn't . . . coming . . . back," she said, her speech breaking. "Face it!"

Years later she confesses, "I stopped facing the truth because he did."

How long would we be paying for Don's sins?

*   *   *   *

What I have learned is that I am not paying for Don's sins. Neither are my children. We are responsible for our own sins. That's what I have to confess and lament. But we seem to have had more than our share of horror and havoc. Is it Don's fault? Where is God, our loving heavenly Father? Does He notice? Does He care?

I saw Jesus on a cross—like a crucifix. I was at the kitchen sink, polishing the stainless steel. Something made me think of Nathan. *Dear God, did You notice? Why didn't You stop him? Do You care?* The vision filled my mind. I saw Jesus drop His head, close His eyes in agony. *Yes, I know. Yes, I love him too. No I didn't stop him. Yes, I know your grief.*

In the Scriptures, Isaiah wrote, "In all [your] distress, he too was distressed."[1]

Today, it is enough.

CHAPTER SEVEN

Deconstruction/ Reconstruction

I cry too much and too often to go to Moody Church, the distinguished church in Chicago named for the famed evangelist Dwight L. Moody. Don and I had attended some church music conferences there and the memories are too familiar, too harsh. *How did it happen that I'm sitting here without him?* I can picture him at the magnificent pipe organ on the right-hand side of the auditorium, pulling out all the stops, changing keys on the last verse of each hymn to lift us heavenward.

On the other hand, I didn't cry enough when I visited the big Presbyterian church downtown. It was too *un*familiar. The organist was hidden from view, up high and away, behind the Gothic pulpit. Too fancy for my "Baptist" eyes. Neither church suited me. I was like Goldilocks trying to find the right porridge, the right chair, the right bed.

The Intercontinental Hotel, home of the Tip Top Tavern, its name blazoned in the atmosphere high above the city, seemed an unlikely spiritual refuge but it proved to be "just right." The hotel was home to the little Assembly of God church in downtown Chicago. Sunday morning always felt like church, so Abigail, Anne and I took the #151 bus down Lake Shore Drive to Michigan Avenue each lonely weekend. The bus ride served a dual purpose, taking us to church and providing me with a vantage point to survey the neighborhood and look for a husband. The girls were my scouts. As the worshipers filed out of the big church on the corner, the fourth stop on the bus route to Lake Shore Assembly, we scanned the crowd for possible candidates—middle-aged men who were alone. I suggested to the girls that we check out this church as an alternative plan some Sunday morning. Abigail reminded me, "Mom, God knows which church we're going to. When He has the right man, he'll be at the right church."

We took the elevator to the tip-top floor of the shabby hotel, hesitated through the long dark hallway, trying to avoid the ragged scuffs in the dirty, dizzying carpet, and seated ourselves at the back, far back, of the enormous "Italian Provincial" dining room metamorphosed into a church. I chose the back row so that I would be far removed from the other worshipers—20 or 30 saints plus me, an adulterous sinner. I stared out the window to avoid making eye contact with anyone. I needed to protect myself, maybe them also. I was so fragile that I thought I might disintegrate if someone came too close and touched me. Here in the back row my tears would not be so conspicuous. Our departure right before the last "Amen" would not be noticed.

This diverse group—doctors, business owners, hair stylists, teens and their parents—invited us into their hotel-church home each week. It was a far cry from the staid Methodist church, the informal Baptist Church, the rigid Baptist church, and our "normal" church. Very small, simple, unpretentious, just church—sing, pray, listen to the message, sing another song. It was sweet and intimate, something I needed even before I knew it.

I had come a long way, baby, having gotten drastically sidetracked along the way. But I could feel something—deconstruction was under way; reconstruction was about to begin. The desperate life I had constructed around my pain was slowly and surely being *de*constructed, and a remodeled, refreshed version of my spiritual life was being *recon*structed. This meant, for one thing, that year by year, for the next few years (reconstruction is not a speedy process), my daughters and I kept moving forward from the back row and getting closer to the front row so that I wouldn't miss any of God and He wouldn't miss any of me.

I had never confessed my adultery out loud to anyone. I suspected that no one knew. *Right.* But one Sunday in June 1988, after the music ended, I was carried by some "spirit" from the front row, my regular spot these days, to the pastor, and I breathed my secret. I asked him to pray for me. A regional business meeting for the brokerage firm was coming up the next weekend—always a convenient trysting time—and I needed a team of wild horses to keep me away, far away.

These business meetings happened every three to four months. A notice would come—"The regional sales meeting is in Cincinnati next month." Or Minneapolis. Or Chicago. They happened all the time, all over the country, in most large corporations. They had been new and exciting for me five years ago when I was a new broker; at these meetings, I crossed the line from purity to depravity. I had relaxed the emotional muscle that supports the ability to say, "No, thank you," or anything that sounded like it. I was an easy target for the smooth old-timers, and not such a reluctant one at that. It didn't matter that it was illicit and immoral; it still felt great.

"What shall I pray about?" my young pastor asked. I thought he would be surprised or shocked when I murmured "adultery." But he wasn't. He didn't tell me to check back with him after I got my act together or when I got my life "cleaned up." He simply smiled and said he would pray. "Let me know if there's anything else I can do for you . . . or your girls."

Could I have stayed away from that business meeting without his prayers, without that little assembly of believers? I don't think so. Maybe someone else could have, but I needed support, connection, care, confession—benchmarks of a satisfying faith community. I wanted people to care for me, and I wanted to care for them. Those are the things that kept me away from the sales meeting that weekend.

I also got some specific care, in the form of some Scripture verses. One of my friends, who often sat next to me in the front row, read to me from Exodus 23. "I have a special word for you," she said: "'See, I am sending an angel ahead of you to guard you along the way and to bring you to the place I have prepared. Pay attention to him. . . . Do not bow down before their [false] gods or worship them or follow their practices.'"[1] I knew that for me, the "practices" were the adulterous affairs I enjoyed at the business meetings. This was a warning and a command. If God was sending an angel to guard me, I had better pay attention.

So instead of going to the sales meeting, I filled the weekend with breakfast, lunch and dinner dates with my women friends. I have notes in my cookbook flagging the "Recipes for Righteousness" that I cooked up. And I have marks in every new Bible highlighting the verses that promised an angel would guard me on my way—my new way.

Don't get me wrong—I still suffered! Staying away was as bad as knowing that James Taylor was in town for a concert but it was sold out and I couldn't get a ticket. I called Sara, my longtime friend in Philadelphia, and wailed, "It's harder to do what's right than what's wrong! This is murder. I want to be with him, to be wanted by him, so much." The flesh puts up a pretty good fight when the Holy Spirit is taking over.

When I told my business colleague/lover that I wasn't going to see him at the sales meeting, that I was going to get back on track with the Lord, he chided, "Oh, come on, you don't have to be *that* holy."

"Oh, that's exactly what I have to be!" I retorted. I gave him back to his wife. And I gave myself back to the Lord. I had chosen lots of substitutes for God's never-failing love. No one measured up, of course. I had "loved" and "been loved" by a line of unsatisfactory lovers, mere men. It took almost seven years for me to discover the difference and close that big heavy door to the darkest side of my life and run to my True Love.

However, behind that big heavy door was one more obstacle to my being a committed, whole-hearted disciple of Jesus Christ. Eliminating my sexual encounters did not change everything. Those affairs were only temporary pain-killers that kept me from dealing with a deeper issue. God was going to have to reconstruct my heart—He was going to have to do the final painstaking work of getting into all the cracks and corners where anger and bitterness had accumulated and hardened. I had a very hard-to-reach corner piled high with almost every severe emotion imaginable—hurt, anger, rejection, sadness, depression, disgust, disbelief, oppression, and on and on. I was not prepared for God's surprising, irresistible blowtorch-healing technique.

In October 1988, Bill Gothard conducted one of his "Basic Life Skills" seminars in Chicago. The seminars are designed for people who are interested in spiritual growth and healing. I had heard about the seminars for years but had never taken the time to attend. One of my friends from church said that she and her son would go with me. Surely there would be something I could pick up there. It turned out to be the final deconstruction of my hard heart.

The conference center was filled with thousands of followers, note-books and Bibles in hand. It didn't matter; I was the only one there. Bill Gothard spoke right to me, as if he had been handed a note earlier in the day alerting him to my condition and had asked everyone else to stay away. Our pastor knew we were going. I truly wondered if he had contacted Gothard during the week before the seminar to give him a heads-up about me.

That night, Gothard was teaching about "A Grateful Heart." Right away I decided this message was *not* for me. Having a grateful heart was the one thing I could *not* have. I did not, I could not, would not have a grateful heart after all that had happened to me. No. No, thank You. Scripture says: "Give thanks in all circumstances."[2] What in the world did that mean?! There are lots of circumstances for lots of people that make those words seem laughable.

I froze. I knew that if I chose to have a grateful heart it would be the same for me as saying to God, "It's okay—everything that has happened to me, everything that You *could* have stopped or changed or rearranged—it's okay. Thank You very much." No. I wasn't even singing most of the songs in church because I thought that if I sang "Holy, holy, holy" it would be admitting that His holiness was more important than my hap-piness. I couldn't admit that. I had to hang on to my hurt and anger and grief. I did not have a grateful heart. I probably never would.

Gothard's message lasted for an hour or so, but what I remember most is a story he told about a sad, angry woman who challenged him at the end of a speech at a previous seminar. The woman had received a phone call from her daughter who was living abroad. The daughter's fran-tic voice begged her mother to come to her immediately—"I think my hus-band is going to kill me!" Before the woman could get there, her daugh-ter's husband had, in fact, killed her. The woman thrust her angry fist at Gothard. "How do you expect me to have a grateful heart after *that!*"

I got it. I mean, I got how angry and helpless she felt. And I got that she could not have a grateful heart. I could cry with her, for her—for me. But I was listening, too. I wanted to hear what Gothard had offered this woman, what he would offer to me, in the way of comfort, sympathy or relief. I wanted to move on with my relationship with God. I had a hunch that my stony heart was a stumbling block to further spiritual growth. It was difficult to swallow the scraps of pain that were stinging my throat. I wanted to weep after hearing the tragic story. *Mr. Gothard, how dare you tell me I need to have a grateful heart! It's easy for my friend Judy to have a grateful heart—her son is alive and well, sitting right here next to her at this seminar, next to me, with us tonight, a charmer just like Nathan, just Nathan's age. And easy for you, Mr. Gothard. You've never even been married, never had children. What do you really know?*

Gothard told us what he said to her: "You must have a grateful heart for the years that you had with your daughter. Be grateful that you had 18 years with her."

It sounded so simple. But what about the loss, the ruin, the finality of the separation? "That's the exact thing I can't do—have a grateful heart," I said to Judy on the way to the car when it was all over. "How can I be grateful?" My heart was breaking all over again. But regardless of the number of years it had taken me to get to Gothard's seminar, it seemed as if the timing was just right.

That same Holy Spirit that drew me to the front of Lake Shore Assembly to ask for prayer in the spring was following me home that autumn night. He helped me—resolute, tearful, grateful—lift and hug Nathan's 12 x 18-inch photograph from the wall in my bedroom and put it beside me on the floor as I knelt by my bed. I couldn't have done it alone. I hadn't been able to do it alone. But that night I had enough encouragement, enough sympathy, enough courage to thank God for the 18 years I'd had my son. I even decided that I could be grateful for my husband. After all, if it weren't for him, I wouldn't have any children. The reconstruction of my heart began on my knees, with Nathan beside me, always smiling, always 18. I could see him through my tears.

I read from the book of Psalms almost every day for two years. I read them on the bus going to work. I wrote them in my journal—every promise, every prayer, seemed to have my name in it. I found my life in the Word of God. The pleadings were mine, the praise was mine, the lessons were mine. I got reacquainted with the words of life.

"I'm back!" I told my young praying pastor. I meant more than "I'm back from the weekend," more than "I'm back on the front row." I meant that my heart was back in the Word, I was back on my knees, back with the precious Holy Spirit.

I had to learn to pray all over again—there hadn't been much inclination to pray when I was wandering in the wilderness. But I found that I didn't know how to pray any more. When I picked up a book about prayer, I felt guilty—I should just be praying, not reading about praying. And then if I went ahead with my reading, I realized that I had failed miserably, so I gave up, thinking that I would never get it quite right. I wondered about everyone else. *Do they really pray like the books tell me to do, or do they fumble and mumble the way I do? Do people really pray alone at sunrise or bedtime or in their "quiet time"? And what do they do, what do they say? And is it all just speaking to the air?*

I desperately wanted to connect with the Lord, the One who is the Everlasting God, the Creator of the ends of the earth. I wanted to feel warm and glow-y when my "quiet time" was finished. I wanted to believe that I had been in touch with the mysterious and overwhelming and magnificent all-glorious God of this universe. And I wanted to know that my prayers were heard and valued and answered—that things would change, that I would change, that my children and my grandchildren and my friends would be beneficiaries of my words spoken in silence in my living room, or on my walk by the lake, or in the shower.

So I tried something new. I decided to talk to God out loud, just the way I would talk to anyone. I began to read my Bible out loud, too, just as if God were in the room, talking to me. I felt connected, engaged, heard. I also began to write down what I was talking about to God while I was saying it so that I had a record of my conversations. I recorded the Scripture verses I read so that I could remember what God said to me. A wise young pastor surprised me by saying, "God has something to say to you every day, so read until the Holy Spirit shines His light on some verse or passage. If you start out by asking Him to say something to you, He will, and that will help you make sense of what's going on in your life." That's when I learned that my life is in the Word.

Especially in the life of Queen Esther: "Who knows but that you have come to the kingdom for such a time as this."[3] This verse has challenged and intrigued me. If my life can be interpreted or explained in the Word of God, then this verse suggests, even dares me, to see every situation as an opportunity for influence, even power.

Esther was pampered and groomed for a year before she would become queen. It sounds very glamorous, but she was actually a prisoner, albeit in a spa environment. She had no control over the events of her life. But she was in the hands of the Living God, getting prepared to be the instrument in His hands that would save her people—His people, the Jews. In that role, she ultimately obtained a royal edict from the king that would set her people free.

How does Esther's life explain my life? Here's what I think: I, too, have come to the kingdom for such a time as this. I have not gone to the spa, but I have been held in God's hands throughout my entire life. Many times it seemed like a prison—I felt hopeless. I had no control over my life or the lives of my family. But God was equipping and preparing me to help save His people. I don't know all of what that means. But I am convinced that I have come to the kingdom for such a time as this.

What kingdom?

I believe that one part of my kingdom is the homosexual community. God has taken me on a journey from fear and anger to love and respect for those living homosexually. I have been morphed, transformed during the last 20 years—it took me a lot longer in the spa routine than it did Esther! But in those 20-plus years I have been given a different heart. I want the gay and lesbian communities to see and hear at least one voice of love and respect—not agreement, not compromise, but love and respect.

Another part of my kingdom is the family, friends and church community of "loved" ones who are in same-sex relationships. I also want this community to see and hear a voice of love and respect—not agreement, not compromise, but love and respect.

When I share my journey with this community, I am in fact issuing a mandate, an edict from the King to set His people free. This means two things: The faith community gets set free from its confusion and paralysis about loving gays, and the gays get set free from our quarantine.

And what time?

The time is now. This is the time for the Church, the Body of Christ, the followers of Christ, to be known by our love. We have separated our-

selves from the gay community long enough, seeing them as our enemies, hating them, disdaining them, judging them. I have been there.
I have done it. I used to say, "Well, because of my experience (with my
husband and his life and death from AIDS), I have every right to ignore
them and despise them. Don't I?" The better truth, God's truth, is that
because of my experience I might be one of the best equipped and prepared to love them. *Much has been given, much is required.*[4] *The one who is forgiven much loves much.*[5]

Well, it's over for me—that judging, condemning, disdaining attitude
is over for me. God has judged *me* and I have been found wanting. He has
shaken me and roused me and disturbed me and convicted me and surprised me. This is the work of the Holy Spirit, making me more like Jesus,
working together in me all of the events of my life to show me what the
Father is doing. The Father is loving, inviting, healing, *loving,* calling,
drawing, *loving.* That's His work that must be lived out in me. I had better get busy.

"I will call them 'my people' who are not my people; and I will call
her 'my loved one' who is not my loved one" and "It will happen
that in the very place where it was said to them 'You are not my
people,' they will be called '[children] of the living God.'"[6]

God is teaching me from those verses, just as He taught Hosea. When
I read them, I believed that they related to the Church and the gay community. (The Bible is not just a Book about what God did; it's a Book
about what He is *doing!*) I—we—have thought that homosexuals were not
"God's people," not "loved" by God. I—we—have believed that this "sin of
all sins," "worst of all sins," was going to keep them eternally separated
from God's love, prevent them from ever being His "people" unless they
became like "us." Our churches are the very places where we have said those
words: *You are not [God's] people.'* Well, hallelujah, God's Word will accomplish what *He* intends—*It will happen that in the very place where it was said to
them 'You are not My people,' they will be called '[children] of the living God.'"*

God burned these verses into my heart and called me to this place of
passion for His Word and for His people—whoever they are—as surely as

He called Moses or Deborah or Esther or David or Daniel or me or—maybe—you. Our responsibility is to go and to tell this message, and to love. Jesus confronts us, challenges us: "The harvest is plentiful, but the workers are few."[7]

Another Heartbreak

I might as well realize that I'm back in the garden—not that first garden, the Garden of Eden, where Adam and Eve ate the apple—but the Garden of Gethsemane, where Jesus prayed the night before He was crucified. I must settle it with God that I will choose His will over mine. I can hardly stand it; I want my will so badly. I'm like Tevye in *Fiddler on the Roof*.

Tevye: "Would it spoil some vast eternal plan, if I were a wealthy man?" (Me: "Would it spoil some vast eternal plan, if You would bring back Anne?")

It started with that phone call in April 1997.

"Hi Mom, it's Anne. I'm calling to tell you I've fallen in love . . . with a woman. I saw her across a crowded room. I've always wondered what love was really like. But this is real. It's wonderful—it happened last week at the *Vanity Fair* party at the Oscars. I wanted to tell you right away because it's going to be very public. Her name is Ellen DeGeneres—you may have heard of her. It's going to be in all the media. I know this is a real surprise for you, Mom. I can't talk now, but I'll call you later and tell you more. Bye, Mom, I love you."

At the time, I had no idea how much this one-way conversation would change our lives—not just Anne's life, but *my* life. I felt angry, anxious and betrayed, crushed and concerned, discouraged and depressed, frustrated and frantic, hopeless and helpless—you get the picture.

And I felt so alone. Surely no other mother—a single mother whose husband, the father of this child, the father who died of AIDS—ever had this happen. I will probably end up in the *Guinness Book of Records*. Anne said this is the best thing that had ever happened to her; I couldn't imagine anything worse right now.

I hung up the phone—in a better place spiritually than when my husband's homosexuality was revealed—and believed that somehow the Lord would help me. I secretly hoped that Anne's affair would last a week or two, maybe a couple of months, certainly not more than a year. That was as long as I thought I could live with another broken heart.

God thought I could last longer than that. Anne and I went through years of on-again, off-again relating—connecting and disconnecting. We worked so hard at holding on to our different "truths." We said that we would stake our lives on them. Really, they only divided us and created a huge gap.

We Connect

January 1998. "Our worlds are so distinct," Anne accuses. "I don't like who I am when I'm with you."

"I feel awkward and scared that I'll say the wrong thing," I confess. "I get paralyzed. I fall so far short of your desire for my wholehearted embrace of your world."

(At least we're talking.)

We Disconnect

End of 1998. "Anne Heche has been named one of *People* magazine's 'Most Beautiful People.'"

(We're not talking.)

We Connect

February 2000. "Mom, come to L.A. for the premiere of my movie! We'll have a great time!" She and Ellen treat me like royalty—new clothes, steak dinners, Pictionary game nights, badminton.

(We're talking!)

We Disconnect

"Anne Heche will star with Vince Vaughn in the remake of Alfred Hitchcock's legendary thriller, *Psycho,* playing the role that Janet Leigh made famous."

(We aren't talking.)

We Connect

"Mom, you have always wanted to be a good mother. Start doing something different and put your family back together," Anne admonishes in a painful phone message.

"Anne, I can't bless your relationship with Ellen," I snap.

(We're talking.)

We Disconnect

Tabloid headlines: "Anne and Ellen Married in Secret Ceremony."

(We're not talking.)

We Connect

"Be our guest," Craig (Anne's and Ellen's wonderful manager) says over the phone. "She's as funny as ever, wanting to get back into the public eye after her television show was canceled. She's on the road with a new stand-up routine."

Ellen is making a comeback! She's going to be in Chicago, May 20, 2000, at the Chicago Theater. Anne documents the tour with the help of cameraman Coley Laffoon (yes, the photographer who later became her husband) and his crew.

"We'll fix up Coley with Susan and Jud's tall, gorgeous blonde nanny," I plot with Anne. We think it's a great idea at the time.

"Can we plan a party?" I ask her. "A birthday celebration for your thirty-first birthday—not downtown, but a dinner here at the house? For everyone—you and Ellen, and your crew? Maybe you'll even want to shoot some footage here at the condo." I want to give and get as much as I can out of this precious time together.

"Great, Mom," Anne answers. "Why don't you cook our favorite spaghetti sauce and have a big salad, and cheesecake for the birthday cake. It's El's favorite. That will make a big hit after a long drive in our tour bus and the big show downtown. By the way, May 20 is Betty's [Ellen's mom] seventieth birthday. Too bad she's not in town."

I jump in. "Let's invite her. She should be here!"

Ellen and Anne are very generous: "Invite as many guests to the show as you would like and we'll meet them after the show if anyone's

interested," comes their message to me. I take advantage of this opportunity to show off my talented daughter. I invite all of Susan's family—
Ellen has always prided herself on family entertainment, so seven-year-
old Ben laughs right out loud with the rest of the audience—and 20
women from my Monday night Bible study.

We never stop laughing. Ellen calls out my name in her routine,
and we get the privilege of going up the dusty back stairs into the
"green room" of the theater. "Elliot!" Anne exclaims to her six-foot
nephew. "I would never recognize you—you have grown a foot since I
last saw you!" Hugs and kisses to the kids who are almost strangers to
their famous aunt.

The "book club" girls shake hands shyly with Anne and Ellen and
smile their thanks. "You are SO funny!" and then turn around and trudge
downstairs and exit through the heavy backstage door. It went down in
history as a night to remember, along with the time we all went to see the
Vagina Monologues. (One of Abigail's friends owned the theater where it was
playing and gave us half-price tickets. *Ummm, thanks, but maybe a little
unusual entertainment for the Bible study group, after all.*)

Abigail and I rush home to get dinner ready. I have prompted my
doorman and garage attendant about the stars' arrival—"Be cool."

Ellen's mom, Betty, has arrived and is the honored guest, along with
Anne. The apartment is full and a little uncomfortable—not because the
space is crowded, and it is—but because we are all walking the invisible
tightrope stretched from the kitchen through the dining room all the
way across the room to the picture windows overlooking the lake.

First I balance on one foot—the happy hostess foot, feeling proud
and grateful; then I step gingerly with the other foot—the hapless
hostage foot, feeling trapped and helpless. We all know what's going on
(well maybe not Ben), and we feel the tension. We celebrate right around
it. It will be the last time I see Anne until . . .

We Connect (Again)

"Hi, Mom. I wanted you to know that I'm making your cheesecake today
for Christmas Eve. Merry Christmas from Ellen and me!"

(*We're talking.*)

We Disconnect

"I'm pregnant!" Anne discloses in a television interview with Barbara Walters. I hear the good news about her pregnancy and my new grandchild along with 25,000,000 other Americans. Later she reveals her gorgeous motherhood in *Mirabella* fashion magazine.

(*We aren't talking.*)

I feel so alienated, disconnected, cheated. Barbara Walters knew before I did. But it's more than that. *How much longer do I have to suffer? Is my time almost up, Lord? Are we there yet?* I sound like I did as a child when I would plead with my father as we traveled the very long 60-mile road trip to my grandparents' house, hoping to arrive before I got car sick again—"Are we there yet?"

*   *   *   *

There is no clear final destination for this trip with Anne. I can hardly imagine the complexity and the pain of the journey—probably for both of us. But I received some clear instructions from the Word of God. Here's what I read:

There was a man who had two sons. The younger one said to his father, 'Father, give me my share of the estate.' So he divided his property between them.

Not long after that, the younger son got together all he had, set off for a distant country and there squandered his wealth in wild living. After he had spent everything, there was a severe famine in that whole country, and he began to be in need. So he went and hired himself out to a citizen of that country, who sent him to his fields to feed pigs. He longed to fill his stomach with the pods that the pigs were eating, but no one gave him anything.

When he came to his senses, he said, "How many of my father's hired men have food to spare, and here I am starving to death! I will set out and go back to my father and say to him: Father, I have sinned against heaven and against you. I am no longer worthy to be called your son; make me like one of your hired men." So he got up and went to his father.

But while he was still a long way off, his father saw him and was filled with compassion for him; he ran to his son, threw his arms around him and kissed him.

The son said to him, "Father, I have sinned against heaven and against you. I am no longer worthy to be called your son."

But the father said to his servants, "Quick! Bring the best robe and put it on him. Put a ring on his finger and sandals on his feet. Bring the fattened calf and kill it. Let's have a feast and celebrate. For this son of mine was dead and is alive again; he was lost and is found." So they began to celebrate.[1]

Of course! I thought. Why didn't I think of this? It's the perfect story for my situation. It's about a rich, impulsive son who leaves his home but eventually follows his broken heart back home.

This is also a story about a wise, merciful brokenhearted father who celebrates the son's homecoming. He's a father full of immense mercy and tender-heartedness—a father who is a picture of what God, our heavenly Father, is like; what Jesus is like. This is a story about an all-loving, all-giving, all forgiving, everything-I-have-is-yours kind of father.

This story was definitely not about me. Would I ever be like that wonderful father?

I thought, *As long as it takes for God to change and heal my broken heart is how long it will take for Anne to come "home." If I can be the father, she will be the son.*

How will my heart change and heal? How long will it take? Will I ever be able to let it all go? Lay it down? Give it up? This might be the place to put into practice what I learned growing up: Don't ask questions. Act as if nothing has happened. Blink once. Blink twice. Blink several times.

Father, make my heart like that father's heart, THE Father's heart. How will You do it? What will it take to melt my heart, heal the anger and hurt, fill me with love and give me a heart that celebrates homecoming and reunion, a heart that blesses? How long will it take to change my heart? How many days, weeks, months, years? How many tears?

Then I heard the words "equipping" and "preparing" in my head. I looked back at the story. When I read it again, I believed that God was going to be equipping and preparing me to be that kind of person. When His work in me was ready, He would bring Anne and me together again. Not until then. God was revealing His heart to me. This was to be the blueprint for my relationship with Anne—and with others.

What was so clear to me about this story of the Prodigal Son was that the story was not about the son, it was about the father. It was about me! The story describes a parent, a spouse, a sister or brother, a child, a friend who has cried oceans of tears, whose heart is broken, but who still stretches out her arms and offers her heart in mercy and tender-heartedness. *WELCOME HOME!* The story describes one who offers to another the same grace that is offered to her. She overlooks, doesn't keep score, expects nothing in return. She is full of extravagant and radical compassion and love.

I wanted to be that kind of person! This is who Jesus is! Nancy, be like Jesus; be like the all-loving, all-giving, all-forgiving, everything-I-have-is-yours kind of person who doesn't measure out your love to others according to how they act or what they believe.

I realized why God had drawn me to that story. It wasn't to focus on the son; it was to understand the Father. He alone could change and heal my broken heart. He alone could equip and prepare me to become like Himself—like the father in the story.

We are invited into the heart of God, invited to look at people and the world through the eyes of God, full of love. I was being drawn into this kind of love. I was being drawn into the heart of God where I could be changed and healed.

I don't remember where I found these words, but they ring true for me: "All of us are caught in the agonies of God's failure to come on our schedule, the hope that we will be saved or healed or rescued without being changed through the painful stretching of our time into God's."

Perhaps theologian Walter Brueggemann says it best: "Hope is the exultant, celebrative conviction that God will not quit until God has had God's full way in my life."

The equipping and preparing process has taken several years—more time than I could have imagined. (So don't expect the "good news" on the next page!)

✳   ✳   ✳   ✳

I taped a quotation from the church program on my microwave:

> *Daughters may spurn our appeals,*
> *Reject our message,*
> *Oppose our arguments,*
> *Despise our persons,*
> ✓ *But they are helpless against our prayers.*

Praying for Anne was to be one strategy that would change and heal my heart. It was difficult to stay angry when I prayed. I felt encouraged every time I read that last line, *But they are helpless against our prayers.* I may never know what Anne got out of those prayers, but I was trusting God that *I* could change.

It is the Word of God that truly changes me. It renews my mind, turns me around and heals me. I knew I would have to search for verses that would give me direction and hope. So I wrestled with God and His Word—on my comfy sofa, in bed, on my bedroom floor, with a box of tissues beside me.

One gloomy hopeless morning, I was looking at some pictures of Anne. I was half kneeling—trying to pray, trying to read through tear-filled eyes—and half lying prostrate—unable to stay upright, falling over, crying my eyes out, trying to reconcile God's plan for my life with His undying love for me. Sometimes it was really hard for me to believe that a loving God had designed *this* plan for my life.

I had cried so much that morning. I can't connect with God—Who is He that allows these things to come into my life? Where is abundant life? I still haven't seen the good that has been worked together in my life from Nathan's death, or Don's life and death, or Anne's estrangement, or Cynthia's short life and death, or Susan's brain cancer, or the many difficult things that have happened in my life. Am I really getting to be more like Jesus?

Today the only connection with Jesus is the knowledge that I am almost as miserable as He was in the Garden of Gethsemane. I opened my Bible to Matthew 26, to read the story. I suddenly realized that my posture was probably similar to His as He cried out to God to do something, to do it some other way. He fell with His face to the ground. He was sorrowful and troubled, overwhelmed with sorrow to the point of death. He prayed, *My Father, if it's possible, may this cup be taken from me.*

I prayed the same thing: "Please stop torturing me. Please may this cup be taken from me. I can't bear this hurt and betrayal any longer."

Then Jesus prayed again, *My Father, if it is not possible for this cup to be taken away unless I drink it . . .*

I couldn't even breathe those words—"If it's not possible?! No! It has to be possible. *Something* has to be possible. Anything but *this!*"

I pulled more tissues out of the box, pressed my face against the pillow and sobbed. I am sorrowful and troubled, overwhelmed with sorrow. I don't mean to compare my suffering to Jesus' suffering, but this is just about as much as I can take.

So He left them and went away once more and prayed the third time, saying the same thing, "My Father, if it is not possible for this cup to be taken away unless I drink it, may Your will be done.

He returned to the disciples and said to them...Rise, let us go!

In His third prayer, Jesus confirms with the Father that this is the Father's will. Jesus heard the Father clearly. The Father had not made a mistake in His plan. *The hour is near. I have come to the kingdom for such a time as this.* Jesus submitted to God's will and His way. And then Jesus was empowered! He took charge of the disciples, the soldiers in the garden, the servant's severed ear, and Judas, his betrayer. Then Jesus acknowledged the goodness of the Father and the truth of His Word to the crowd. He reminded them: *Do you think I cannot call on my Father and He will at once put at my disposal more than twelve legions of angels? But how then would the Scriptures be fulfilled that say it must happen in this way?*

That morning, when I looked at the words on the page, I heard these words in my head: *He settled it. He settled it that He would do it God's way.*

I realized this was the only way for me, too. I had to settle it with God that I would be willing for His will in my life. It was very clear to me: *Not as I will, but as You will.* I could not—and He *would* not—change the circumstances of my life right now.

When I settled it, I stopped choking and blowing and sniffling. I sat up with my Bible, squared myself with my back against my bed—my knees propped up to hold my Bible—and looked again at the verses.

I know I'm not Jesus, but I got the same message. My Father could send twelve legions of angels to change my life, to rescue me, to deliver me from whatever, but *it must happen in this way.*

Okay. I choose to settle it with God and I will trust Him whether I agree with Him or not, whether I understand my circumstances or not, whether I like it or not. And I choose to believe that I will be empowered with Holy Spirit power that is beyond my understanding.

I pushed the button on my CD player and waited to hear the song "The Potter's Hand."

Beautiful Lord, wonderful Savior, I know for sure
all of my days are held in Your Hand, crafted into Your perfect plan. . . .[2]

*   *   *   *

When Anne announced her intention to live homosexually, I felt hurt and angry; alone and afraid. I had no one to talk to, and Anne and I couldn't find any common ground on which to communicate so that we could help each other. One day, when we were on the phone together, I said: "I think you love Ellen in the same way that I love Jesus," thinking that we could understand each other's passion and connect around "love."

It ended up sounding like an accusation or an insult, I guess. Anyway, it didn't help us get closer.

Most of the family members and friends I meet who talk about their loved ones who are in same-sex relationships want to do just that—get closer, even in the midst of confusion and pain. They don't know if they *should,* or if it's *okay,* or if it's *God's will* to pursue a relationship with their loved one. And then we wonder about the entire gay community. What should we do? What *can* we do?

I think Jesus gives some insight on what to do in Matthew 26. His first prayer is *My Father, if it is possible, may this cup be taken from me. Yet not as I will, but as You will.* The sense of this in the Greek is that the "cup" would pass by Him without His having to drink it. It's almost as if Jesus would be able to wave the cup away with a brush of His hand. He would be indifferent to it, would not have to take it in.

His next prayer is very different. *My Father, if it is not possible for this cup to be taken away unless I drink it, may Your will be done.* The sense of this prayer in the Greek is that the cup must be taken and drained to the last drop. He must partake fully in drinking the contents of the cup.

Here's what I think this means for me, for us, who are faced with life-changing decisions around our involvement with some of the issues of homosexuality. We can ask that the cup be taken from us. We can turn away, brush it off, be unresponsive, act as if we could change the situation by ignoring it. We can refuse to engage and interact with our loved ones out of fear, anger, hurt or confusion.

Or we can do the opposite.

Bruxy Cavey, teaching pastor at The Meeting House in Toronto, wrote:

> We should be pouring our active energies into the "we love you" message. . . . We should find practical ways to serve the gay community, always showing them the utmost respect as image-bearers of God. If we do this rightly, we will be living the counter-cultural lifestyle that Jesus holds out for us. We will be that unique Kingdom society within our secular culture that shows the world how to bless those whom we do not agree with and who may not agree with us . . . pour our energies into organizing our voice to offer a message of love and life to our world via the Gospel.[3]

We do not have to be confused any longer. We can do what we see the Father doing, what Jesus is doing. Jesus drinks the cup. He is fully engaged in the difficult, painful, life-giving, life-changing process. We can follow Jesus. We can drink the cup to the last unfamiliar drop. We may get crucified. We may get rebuffed and rejected. We may not see any light at the end of the tunnel. But if we follow Jesus, we're in good company.

Drink up, I say—drink to the last drop!

*   *   *   *

Journal entry
February 11, 2004, 7:49 a.m.

I saw the sun get up today. I knew it was coming. I saw a pink line across the horizon while the rest of the sky was still dark. I can look out of my windows on the seventh floor of my high-rise condo building and look right out across the lake and see where the day begins. If you live in the woods or down in the city where buildings block the horizon, you don't get to see where the day really begins. When you look up and see the sun from there, you know the day actually started a long time ago.

It's very important to know that the sun will come up every day. For me it is life-giving. I know that the sun will—no doubt about it, absolutely, definitely, just-wait-and-I'll-show-you—come up and then I know that God can be counted on. At the very least I know He is going to make the sun come up, or, to be exact, the earth turn. That is basic to my faith. Faith is being sure of what you hope for and confident of what you do not see.

Some mornings I don't see the big red ball rise up from the lake— it's cloudy or foggy. But the day gets brighter and the lights that line Lake Shore Drive dim and the cars turn off their headlamps and the runners along the lakefront change from silhouettes of black and gray to lively images of blue and green and yellow. I know the sun has taken over the day. I'm sure of it. Confident of what I do not see.

Today the pink line began to spread and blossom like a big puffy peony, fuller and pinker and more lovely every second, in slow motion. I couldn't detect a single movement and yet it was changing right before my eyes. I knew exactly where the shocking rock of sun would appear because the color intensified in that spot. And then it was there, a sliver, peeking shyly at first, slowly and evenly. The whole sun is in view, filling its magnificent preordained space right outside my window. Sometimes like a marionette on a string that has only a bit part in the performance it is slowly and silently pulled up out of view into a curtain of clouds. But what a performance! And what promise fulfilled. And what faith satisfied.

I have to count on God for a lot of things. I have searched my Bible for promises that I could believe and hope in for my family, my career, my finances, my relationships. I made a decision to trust God for those things, believing that He would come through in the same way that I know without a doubt that the sun will come up.

I don't get a promise fulfilled every day as regularly as sunrise! I waited several years to see what would happen in Anne's relationship with Ellen. I hoped for Abigail and Joe's second marriage to go well and it didn't. I wanted a position at Moody Church that I thought was perfect for me, and I was turned down. I begged for Susan's brain tumor to be healed and so far it hasn't been. I hoped for a long and happy marriage.

So how do I reconcile these things, these disappointments, and many others, with still being able to count on God? I regroup. I reread. I study my Bible to see what part my keeping-my-fingers-crossed kind of hope I had—imposing my wish for a specific time and place and outcome over God's later or other time, and bigger or different place and plan.

I resolve to find God's perspective. I choose to not doubt His good intentions for me. I am committed to knowing that the sun will rise and that God will show me the fulfillment of His promise in a slow-motion, unfolding, blossoming kind of way. I might not even see it right away. It might make a brief appearance and then fade away for a while. But the day gets brighter. My heart is lighter. I am reminded in my heart that there is hope and certainty, and I trust again.

When I'm on the other side of the lake, I can watch the sun go down (the Earth turn). Very slowly, predictably it takes its bow, drops into the horizon like a coin into a silk-lined pocket, surrounded by the silent splendor of pink and purple and blue and violet in celebration of a day well done. It seems to rest. And yet it rises for another, far away, who is hoping with all her heart that the sun will appear to begin her day and satisfy her faith.

CHAPTER NINE

My Hard Heart

God showed me my hard heart in Los Angeles—the City of Angels—right in the midst of a visit with my daughter, right in the midst of her lesbian affair. It was the spring of 2000. I was there to celebrate her, to join with hundreds of people in the "industry" to honor her work as a writer and a director. Anne had accomplished what few young twenty-something women have done—she wrote a story, sold the concept to HBO, made the deal and directed the made-for-television movie with two powerful stars, Ellen DeGeneres and Sharon Stone. I was privileged to be part of the enthusiastic crowd that included Maria Shriver and Arnold Schwarzenegger, singer Melissa Etheridge and her girlfriend, and superstar musician Michael Bolton, among others.

It's really hard for me to have a hard heart—aching, occupied with self-righteousness—in the midst of all that excitement, all that achievement and success; amidst all the glamour and hype that Hollywood can bestow. Hooray for Anne! Kudos, high fives, congratulations! You're amazing! What's not to celebrate!

I once heard a marriage counselor say that men are like waffles and women are like spaghetti: Men compartmentalize things and issues so that they don't overlap, and women tangle things together so that they can hardly be distinguished from one another. That night, I wished I could divide my heart like a waffle into tiny perfect little compartments. One for my biblical Christianity; one for each child and her life; one for my friends and their opinions and suggestions; one for my therapist; one for career; one for leisure; one for grandchildren—you know, so that Jesus doesn't get tangled up with my therapy or my career or my children or a celebration of my extremely talented daughter who is living homosexually and has just produced a movie about a lesbian couple who want to have a child.

But I am not a waffle; I am spaghetti. I am tangled up emotionally. I am troubled, conflicted. I am pretty much in a continual fume of grief about how to reconcile Anne's decision to live homosexually with my unwavering though unspoken vow that our family will have nothing to do with the homosexual community. Remember what we had suffered as a result of my husband's life and death with AIDS! Was I the only one who still recoiled from that humiliation? That devastation? Sometimes I think I must be walking in my sleep or dreaming—it seems so unlikely that my daughter is involved in a lesbian affair.

But it's not just that—that wasn't the only hard part. It was also hard for me to see the daughter who had once committed her young life to following Christ now live a blatant denial of that commitment. I was angry about that, angry at her for breaking that vow as well. It felt as if her new life was a personal affront to me, an insult to me, intended to hurt me. And I *was* hurt and angry. It seemed as if my celebrating her, celebrating her work, would compromise me, would destroy my "testimony." How would I reconcile my staunch convictions with her opposition to them and still maintain a loving relationship with my daughter? I couldn't figure it out.

On one hand, I wanted to be a worthy, righteous and holy disciple, standing boldly for the "truth." That meant—I *thought*—that I needed to separate myself emotionally, if not physically, from anything having to do with homosexuality, that I needed to make myself aloof and distant, however confusing and difficult it was. I wouldn't watch Ellen's sitcom. I wouldn't cheer their highly publicized encounter with (then) President Bill Clinton. When I walked by newsstands where tabloids were proclaiming Anne and Ellen's marriage or wanting to have a baby, I would hurry by. Having caught a glimpse of their names and pictures, I could feel my heart sink and my eyes burn with tears. I would pick up my pace, hoping no one would see me, or wishing that everyone would see me and know my pain and feel sorry for me.

On the other hand, I wanted to be like the priest in Hebrews 5:1-2:

Every high priest [that's us, as believers in Christ] is selected . . .
and is appointed to represent [the people] in matters related to
God, to offer gifts and sacrifices for sins. [S]he is able to deal gently with those who are ignorant and are going astray, since [s]he
[her]self is subject to weakness.

That's me. I've been ignorant and I've gone astray. I'm subject to
weakness. Who am I to set myself up as some holier-than-thou example
of obedience and morality?! Why should I single out this sin as *the* one
to break our relationship? My sins are simply different. I should be like
Job (see Job 1:5), like the priest, representing my children to God, offering gifts and sacrifices for sin, dealing gently with them. That's what
I wanted to do. But I have not dealt gently.

What I have learned over the last few months is that even though
many biblical Christians—and I speak for myself as well—have isolated
homosexuality as the *worst* sin listed in the first chapter of Romans, it is
not singled out as number one. The Bible presents it in "good" company along with many other sins, such as "greed" and "lust" that are committed by all of us from time to time when we "also suppress the truth
by [our] wickedness." I find myself in Romans, chapter 1, as well, along
with the homosexuals. Although I know God, I do not always glorify
Him or give Him thanks; my foolish heart has been dark; I claim to be
wise but am often a fool; I have given myself over to sexual impurity;
I have worshiped the created rather than the Creator; I have been filled
with lust and greed and envy and gossip and malice and slander and dis-
obedience and strife and deceit and arrogance; I am senseless, faithless,
heartless, ruthless, stubborn and unrepentant—and at the same time
condemn these things in others. Worst of all, I have shown contempt for
the riches of God's kindness, tolerance and patience toward other sinners, not realizing that God's kindness leads us to repentance. I have
wanted Him to *do* something, quickly, to those other sinners.

How dare I—really!—how dare I wave a banner or carry a big card
protesting homosexuality. Why not a banner protesting greed or gossip
or envy or hard-heartedness? Mike Haley, a friend from Focus on the
Family's Love Won Out conference, a man who lived homosexually for

more than 10 years, tells a story of a time when he attended a church service where he and several others who were coming out of homosexuality
into a committed life of obedience to God were asked to come to the
front of the church for prayer. Members of the congregation came with
them to offer support. It was a heart-warming scene. But when Mike
talks about it, he suggests that it might be a good idea to dedicate a
prayer time some Sunday to the gossips.

But homosexuality *seems* worse.

*   *   *   *

The night of the big event began with a limo caravan, a red carpet
arrival at the theater (just like I've seen on the night of the Oscars),
smiles and waves and interviews a block long, the showing of Anne's
film, and shouts of congratulations when the credits rolled. It began
like any other sunny day in southern California. Makeup artists and
wardrobe designers stampeded Anne and Ellen's gorgeous home. Long-
stemmed white French tulips—Anne's favorite—were delivered by the
truckload. Caterers covered the Spanish courtyard around the pool
with elegant tables of elegant food. Friends who shared the excitement
as well as the success of getting such a controversial film produced by a
major network arrived with two thumbs up, way up.

Anne and Ellen bought me a luscious silk Jil Sander V-necked sweater
and long chiffon skirt for the occasion. I, of course, had spent several days
at home agonizing over what to wear. I lugged a suitcase full of everything
from casual, and dressy casual, to cocktail, mid-calf formal and floor-
length formal choices, plus half a dozen pairs of shoes to match. My
designer friend Maria, who worked at the Chanel boutique in Chicago,
loaned me a dress that seemed perfect, but who knew for sure? While the
crowd in the 500-square-foot dressing room upstairs sharpened Anne and
Ellen for show time, I brushed on my own makeup in Midwestern fashion
and slipped into my ensemble in my sumptuous suite downstairs.

I wasn't pretending—I was as proud as any mother could be, and as
charming as anyone, almost. I smiled and shook hands and toasted the

stars with confidence. I stayed by Anne's side, the side opposite from Ellen, and beamed my pride right back to the fans.

The HBO executives created a glamorous party pavilion across the street from the theater that mesmerized the partygoers. We floated into a tinsel-town fantasyland—champagne fountains, elaborate mountains of food, cool live music, and fireworks—after the movie. I can't describe the ambivalence in my un-compartmentalized heart. I wanted to jump up and down with joy as well as fall to my knees in sadness. *This is not my world. I feel so lost and out of place. But I'm her mother, she's my very own precious daughter—I do belong here. Somebody help me!*

The next day in my hotel room, reading my Bible, I came across a verse that exploded like the burst of fireworks from the night before—full of surprise and splendor: "God was reconciling the world to Himself in Christ, not counting men's sins against them, and He has committed to us the message of reconciliation."[1]

That verse convicted me. It "outed" me. Oh, I wasn't having a secret homosexual affair. I wasn't picketing and protesting, waving a banner or carrying a big sign. But I had a big sign all right. I carried it in my hard heart, with the word "homosexual" scrawled across it. Every time I thought about my husband or my daughter, I held up my big card and waved my ugly sign. I counted that sin of homosexuality against them.

My hard heart had created a huge gap in my relationship with my daughter (and with her friends). We tried, she tried, I tried, to talk about my schoolwork, her projects, her sisters and her nieces and nephews, but we always ended up arguing about our disagreements and convictions. We couldn't agree to disagree. We were both so adamant about our beliefs. So the conversations became more abusive and the distance grew greater, every word eroding the edge of the cliff on which our relationship teetered. We ended with her saying that she never wanted to talk to me again. Then she would call, unexpectedly, a year or so later, out of the blue, and we would begin the whole process over again.

I saw a picture in my mind of something like the Grand Canyon. I'm on one side (the heterosexual side, if you please) with a large, proud, familiar heterosexual crowd. She's way across the canyon on the side with a smaller but nonetheless proud homosexual crowd.

My hard heart keeps me inaccessible and unapproachable to anyone on the far side of that great canyon between us.

How will we ever be able to close the gap—the avowed heterosexual mother and the avowed homosexual daughter?

It occurred to me that this heterosexual/homosexual canyon scenario was not just my problem. Yes, it was about me and my daughter, but it was also about all of us proud heterosexual, Bible believers on that one far side of the canyon separating ourselves from the homosexuals—believers or not—on the far side.

Who would stand in the gap? In the Hebrew Scriptures, the prophet Ezekiel hears these words from the Sovereign Lord: "I looked for [someone] who would . . . stand before me in the gap on behalf of the land so I would not have to destroy it, but I found none."[2]

When the Israelites were wandering and complaining in the wilderness on their way to the Promised Land, Moses stood in the gap—he negotiated before God on behalf of the Israelites—many times: "He said He would destroy them—had not Moses, His chosen one, stood in the [gap] before Him to keep His wrath from destroying them."[3]

What are we doing?! Why am I—why are we—not standing in the gap? Why are we comforting ourselves with our safe but unapproachable friends on one side of the canyon when others *whom we do not want to see "destroyed"* stare incredulously and defensively from the other side? When will I stand in the gap? When will I become a negotiator, a chosen one, to stand in the gap before God, before the gay community, so that *we* are not destroyed? I think this may be the appropriate time to quote Pogo, the famous cartoon character who said, "We have met the enemy, and he is us."

*   *   *   *

I have plans for you. I am reading my old journals to see if I've written anything over the last 10 or 15 years that is relevant to the writing of this book, and I come across the words written February 21, 1999: *I have plans for you. It really doesn't have anything to do with school—school's okay, fine—but it has to do with you.* (In February 1999, I am in my first year of my doctorate program at Northwestern. Anne and Ellen are still together.) *You stand between the living and the dead and make "atonement" for them. . . . You are a priest. . . . You minister the healing ritual, you offer the incense that stops the plague.*

Whatever those words mean, whoever the living and dead are, the words are too closely connected with what I thought was my *new* passion about standing in the gap not to be stunned by them. These words and phrases "stand between," "make atonement," "priest," "healing ritual," "stop the plague," pound in my ear. Perhaps God has been calling me to this place for a long time. Maybe it's God's heart being revealed to me in 1999 and again in 2006 and long ago in 1953, and any number of times—different times, same message.

I look at the verse in 2 Corinthians 5:19 again. "God was reconciling the world to himself in Christ, not counting men's sins against them. And He has committed to us the message of reconciliation."

I take God at His Word. If He says that He has committed to us the message, the ministry of reconciliation, then that means that I am a messenger of the message of reconciliation. I believe that God has brought the issue of homosexuality into my family (and perhaps into *yours*) in order to make my "ministry," my life, my place of serving very clear. He shows me the first part of the verse to convict me and then gives me the second part to show me what repentance looks like (how I am to turn around and go in the other direction). It's very clear: I must commit myself to the message and ministry of reconciliation.

In Isaiah 58, we read that we are blessed with all kinds of promises from the Lord—light that breaks forth like the dawn, healing, glory, satisfied needs, strength. And we are challenged with all kinds of responsibilities—rebuilding the ancient ruins, raising up age-old foundations, *repairing the gaps*, restoring homes.

I don't know exactly what that might look like for you. But for me it means that I break free, walk down into that great canyon and up the other side to make friends, to stand in the gap, to negotiate the love of God that is "not counting [this particular] sin against [the gay community]" as a whole or against any individual who struggles with same-sex attraction, or even against any individual who has given up the struggle and is totally engaged in living homosexually, marrying her/his partner, adopting children, birthing children—whatever.

It means that I stop separating the world into two worlds, the heterosexual and the homosexual, when I read John 3:16, and I read it truthfully: "God so loved *the whole world—all the people in the world—*that He gave His one and only Son that whoever believes in Him shall not perish but have eternal life."

It means that I "go and make disciples of all the world [not two separate worlds]."[4]

It means that I "do not forget to entertain strangers, for by so doing some people have entertained angels without knowing it."[5]

It means that I stop living my life with an "us v. them" worldview. And I *stop* holding the gay community hostage to my judgment and condemnation. I live like Jesus, not counting their sins against them every time I think about it.

Buxby Cavey writes

> The truth about "us" and "them" is that there is no "them." There is only "us." We are all beautiful and precious people, infinitely valued by God. We are also all sexually broken people to one degree or another, needing the healing of authentic community to live as Jesus calls us to live.[6]

In an article in the *New York Times,* John Leland describes a "new cultural approach for conservative Christians"[7] in which he analyzes various movie reviews and interviews written by conservative Christians regarding the movie *Brokeback Mountain,* a movie about a love affair between two gay cowboys.

In the article, Robert Johnson, a professor at Fuller Seminary in Pasadena, California, says that he believes that "this critical ambivalence [about the movie and about conservative Christians actually viewing the movie] represents a change in the way conservative Christians engage popular culture. . . . Evangelicals as a group are becoming more sophisticated in their interaction with popular culture."[8]

When I read the article, I thought, *Oh, good for us. We're so sophisticated now that we can review a movie about gay men. We sit on our side of the canyon and watch a movie about a homosexual love affair, but will we interact with the gay community itself?* We call it "popular culture." It sounds like a disease, not like real live people—human beings made in the image of God. We can now interact with "popular culture," some impersonal entity far away on the silver screen, but that's as close as we get. It's like so many spice jars in my kitchen cupboard. I take them out and use them once in a while, wipe off the little jars and then put them back and close the door. There, you see? I have interacted with "popular culture." Or maybe it's like bowling. I might do it every two or three years with my grandchildren on a vacation spree, but I probably won't join a bowling league. Maybe once in a while I'll run into a gay man at the hair salon or at Marshall Field's or at a lot of different places. I can be pleasant and engaging. And of course, so can he. There—I've interacted with "popular culture." How sophisticated we are! (It's still a huge gap.)

It has taken more than 20 years, I hasten to add, for me to cross that canyon. I am moving from one edge of the canyon to the other—from a hard heart full of fear, anger and resentment—holding the sins of others against them and adding them to some invisible ledger—with a softer heart that is growing in love and respect. To do that, I needed God to melt my hard heart.

When I read the verse in 2 Corinthians and realized that God, in Christ, is doing the heavenly work of reconciling the world to Himself, with us as His earthly workers, the truth of it melted my hard heart. I was to be part of the solution, not part of the problem.

I believed that God was saying to me that I am a messenger of the message of reconciliation. I am to be like Jesus, not counting people's sins against them, not counting my husband's or my daughter's sins against them, every time I thought of them.

Run, Nancy! Run to the other side of the canyon and take as many people with you as you can! Stand in the gap, fill it up—way up.

CHAPTER TEN

Blessing

My friend and neighbor in Michigan, Sue, who is a new follower of Jesus and was a diligent seeker of truth for many years, asked me if I thought God could or would speak to her. She had a hunch that what she heard in the shower one day was the Lord's "voice" and wanted me to confirm it. I said, "Let's hear it, and maybe that will help us decide."

I know that God speaks to us in the Scriptures, but I also know that I have "heard" words and phrases in my head that I'm sure were God's thoughts. After all, He says in Proverbs 1:23 that He will pour out His heart to me and make His thoughts known to me.

The verses that convince me that God, who dwells in heaven as well as in my humble soul, chooses to reveal Himself to me—yes, speak to me—are a great comfort and boost to my sagging spirit. "'No eye has seen, no ear has heard, no mind has conceived what God has prepared for those who love Him'—*but God has revealed it to us by His Spirit.*"[1]

Thank You.

Jesus, in His prayer recorded in John 17, prayed, "Righteous Father, though the world does not know you, I know you, and they know that you have sent me. *I have made you known to them, and will continue to make you known* in order that the love you have for me may be in them and that I myself may be in them."[2]

Awesome.

Today I'm not sure how much I know about God, but this verse gives me confidence that pretty soon Jesus will reveal more of God to me, by His Spirit; maybe through His Word; maybe by a worship song from Hillsong Church in Australia; maybe through an e-mail from my pastoral friend Sam Storms in Kansas City; maybe in a still, small undeniable impression in my heart and mind.

So here's what Sue told me about hearing God's voice: She was in the shower, moaning about her children, about her life. Her unmarried daughter was pregnant again, by the same man who was the father of her four-year-old son. Their relationship was on again, off again, and Sue was feeling discouraged and hopeless. Sometimes the couple lived together in Sue's home with her family; sometimes they stayed at the boyfriend's house with his other two children from another relationship. Sue's teenage niece and nephew were living with her also. Sue was a full-time wife, mother, aunt and grandmother, and was running a business with two associates. Everyone was already overwhelmed and overloaded. Now this. What were they thinking?! Where was there room for a new baby? It seemed as if this baby would come into the world with a lot of strikes against him. *All the more reason to love him,* was what Sue heard in the shower.

Now tell me, would anyone but God say something like that? *All the more reason to love him.* Think about it, think about that statement, that God-breathed statement that could be said a hundred times over in almost any seemingly burdensome situation to any one of us at any time. Doesn't it sound just like something God would say? I told her I was sure that God was speaking to her. Of course, she already was pretty sure of it. She knew it wasn't something *she* would say, nor would her husband, nor would even her best friends, Fran and Rose, and the other Sue. That was God's heart revealed to her by the precious Spirit of God.

My only question to her was, "Who's the 'him' in the '*All the more reason to love him*'? The father, or the baby?" Exactly. God's word can be specific *and* vague. Of course I have to believe that it's both—all the more reason to love the father *and* the baby. And I will vouch for Sue today, five or six years later—she loves the beautiful boy *and* his father. They are well loved, easy to love actually; and the father has now become the husband of the mother of these two charming boys in a beautiful ceremony with all the children, and a Christ-follower, recently baptized at Cherry Beach in Lake Michigan. *All the more reason to love him!*

Is this the end of a beautiful love story? I doubt it. And they lived happily ever after? Well, I hope there will be moments of great joy, but we can be pretty sure there will be moments of great sadness, too. Really, it goes with the territory. It's life.

Why is so much required of us, of all of us? Will Sue really have enough love, or will she run out? What does God mean when he says that we will not be given more than we can bear?[3] How close to the edge of my endurance will He push, or pull? Tribulation works patience and builds character.[4] Isn't there some other way?

In the book of Judges, Gideon, an Israelite whose family and people are being ravaged and impoverished by foreigners from the land of Midian, encounters an angel at his family's winepress. The angel comes and sits down under a nearby oak tree. "The LORD is with you, mighty warrior," the angel greets Gideon.

"But sir," Gideon replies, "If the Lord is with us, why has all this happened to us? Where are all His wonders that our fathers told us about?"[5]

Yes, I have asked the same thing. Why has all this happened to us? Where are the miracles, the answers to "powerful and effective prayer"[6] that James promises in his writings? Where is the Lord?

What does He want from me? (Don't even answer that.) I know what He wants—He wants everything, He wants it all. He wants me—all of me. And because I don't know how to give it, or I don't want to give it, this is how He works it out, makes it happen. He takes my heart in His hands and, with a firm grip, never letting go for one millisecond, guides me, teaches me, leads me, supports me and trains me in His Way. He speaks to me.

What does He say when trouble comes? What is God's perspective on the suffering we go through? Really, I want to know. I want to believe that there is a plan, a bigger picture, a method in the madness. Gil Grissom, the head of the crime lab team in the television series *CSI: Crime Scene Investigation*, tells investigator Sara Sidle that the reason she gets stuck in her investigation is that she looks at only one piece of evidence, one piece of the puzzle. He on the other hand can see the whole picture.

I'm like Sara. That's me. That's me when I'm stuck in self-pity and frustration. I can see only what's in front of me. I can feel only the sting of the moment. I can't stand back far enough to get God's perspective, to see the whole picture. I'm right in the middle of it, feeling hopeless and angry, not a plan in sight.

From my apartment on Lake Shore Drive in Chicago, I can look out my picture windows and see all of a blue or cloudy or starry or sunny heaven and a seemingly endless sparkling or raging and ever-changing Lake Michigan. I think God is there, in the heavens, in the clouds. I see the Holy Spirit moving in the water and in the mist that hovers over the ice in the winter. But I see only one piece of the picture, literally one drop in the bucket of all of God's creation. I can see only what's in front of me. It's only the smallest smidgen of His vast creation.

Speak to me. Change my perspective. Renew my mind. Help me! Teach me. Tell me why. Why does bad stuff happen to good people? Why does good stuff happen to *bad* people?

And then I hear:

Why do you say, [Nancy], and complain, [Nancy], "My way is hidden from the LORD; my cause is disregarded by my God?" Do you not know? Have you not heard? The LORD is the Everlasting God, the Creator of the ends of the earth, . . . his understanding no one can fathom. He gives strength to the weary and increases the power of the weak. Even youths grow tired and weary, and young men stumble and fall; but those who wait and hope in the LORD will renew their strength. They will soar on wings like eagles; they will run and not grow weary, they will walk and not be faint.[7]

Okay. I confess. I have complained. I have thought that God has forgotten me, yes, forsaken me. And surely I do not understand Him or His ways. If I keep waiting and hoping, and waiting and waiting some more, will I really not faint? Can I trust You? Can I really get what is promised?

Paul says to the Romans:

The promise comes by faith, so that it may be by grace. . . . Against all hope Abraham in hope believed. . . . Without weakening in his faith . . . he did not waver through unbelief regarding the promises of God, but was strengthened in his faith and gave glory to God, being fully persuaded that God had power to do what He had promised. [These words] were written . . . also for us, . . . for us who believe.[8]

Incredible. Thank You.

I am reminded again, or maybe it's for the first time—or at least it seems like the first time—that I know He works together all of the things of my life to make me more like Jesus. The Greek words "work together" mean to be a fellow worker, to cooperate, to collaborate, to be a companion. It's not just that God waves a magic wand over my troubles and *abracadabra!* it's all better. It's God and Nancy working together. He does His work—holding, illuminating, guiding—and I do my work—praying, reading His Word, obeying—and I grow and heal and learn to wait and be patient, and then I become more like Jesus.

When trouble comes, my daughter Abigail coaxes me: "Mom, remember you told me a long time ago that when you were a new believer you prayed that verse, 'to know Christ and the power of His resurrection and the fellowship of sharing in His sufferings, becoming like Him.'"[9]

She said that to me most recently when my oldest daughter, Susan, was diagnosed with brain cancer. *NoNoNoNo.* Why is *this* happening? *What* is this all about?

"Mom, remember that prayer you prayed a long time ago, the one about the fellowship of Christ's suffering?" Abigail said.

I didn't even want to tell my friends that Susan had brain cancer. Most of them thought that already I had gone through enough stuff with my family. And it was absolutely impossible to believe anyway. I would try to put the words together—Susan/brain cancer, Susan/brain cancer. They didn't fit. I could not believe that she would have her brilliant mind eaten away by some insidious, unseen, unknown evil. I would not give up another child. I was going to see her become a grandmother. There is a blessing for me in Psalm 128 that I would see my children's children and their children. I was enjoying Susan's growth as a booming success in her own "dot-com" business, a whole new venture for her creative genius.

I would not, could not do this. How could *she* do it?! We thought we were finished with the hard battles. We had already run the race, run many races. When would we ever be finished?

"It's not fair!" *Not fair?* Leif Enger in his beautiful book *Peace Like a River*, writes, "Fair is whatever God wants to do."[10]

"God will always prune those things that we slavishly seek first, love most and begrudge giving up."[11] This truth, which comes from Bruce Wilkinson's *Secrets of the Vine*, stabs my heart. Is Susan's brain cancer more "pruning"? For me, for her, for all of us? Is this about "bearing much fruit"? Wilkinson goes on to say that a "test of faith doesn't really test anything unless it pushes you past your last test. . . . If you pull back when you reach what seems like your limit, you will never grow or know how much you can *really* trust God."[12] No pain, no gain, in other words.

Okay.

But I cannot imagine Susan's children without their mother. Please, *please* don't let this happen to her children. I might have managed to develop some perseverance and character—borne some fruit through some suffering in my life. I have gained some hope and trust that God has a plan. *There is a bigger picture,* I would say to myself. *There is light at the end of the tunnel.* But not my grandchildren; they do not, cannot, *must* not be asked to do this. How will they ever manage this?

I didn't want anyone to say anything to me. I didn't want books or verses or clichés, especially not spiritual clichés. I knew them all. I had heard them all. I hated them. After all, I had said them all to others over the years: *You're like a modern-day Job. God works everything together for good. Everything's going to be okay. You're so strong, you're the only one I know who can handle it.*

I thought if anyone said those things to me I would scream.

Finally, I did scream. I cried and yelled and screamed at God and told Him I would not do this. Period. I would not do this. *This is more than I can bear. Don't You get it? THIS IS MORE THAN I CAN BEAR.*

Is this what I was being prepared for when I sang those songs and prayed those prayers about the fellowship of Christ's sufferings? *Did You take me at my word, really?* I didn't mean it to happen this way. And why me? Why Susan? Why our family? What have we done? What will we *do*?

But today when I looked at the verse (to know Christ and the power of His resurrection and the fellowship of sharing in His sufferings, becoming like Him), instead of the "suffering" part, I saw the "power" part. That's it. That's how we make it through all the difficult times. Natalie, my brilliant 17-year-old granddaughter said, "Of course, we'll just do it." God has let us experience the power of Christ's resurrection. The power that raised Jesus from the dead is working in us! Paul prayed for that power to be known by the Ephesian believers:

> I keep asking that the God of our Lord Jesus Christ, the glorious Father, may give you the Spirit of wisdom and revelation, so that you may know Him better. I pray also that the eyes of your heart may be enlightened in order that you may know the hope to which He has called you, the riches of His glorious inheritance in the saints, and His incomparably great power for us who believe. That power is like the working of His mighty strength, which He exerted in Christ when He raised Him from the dead.[13]

I have often wondered what that resurrection power—that mighty, divine, life-giving strength working in me—would be like. What would I be able to do if *resurrection power* were alive and well in *me?* Would I be able to move through the suffering, count it all joy, pray without ceasing, praise Him with every breath? Looking back at Philippians 3:10, I see that the power comes *before* the sharing in His sufferings. He has prepared and equipped me so that my feeble knees will hold me up, my tears won't drown me and my feet will take another step. It may not look quite like I've been raised from the dead, but it feels like it. Watching my oldest daughter wear away, watching her children care for her, watching others grieve with us—it was resurrection power.

*   *   *   *

What does God say when trouble comes? In George Macdonald's wonderful allegory *At the Back of the North Wind,* the young hero, Diamond, is lifted out of his lonely bedtime loft by the beautiful and enticing North Wind. "Fear invaded his heart," MacDonald writes. "Diamond, dear," [North Wind] says, "Be a man. What is fearful to you is not the least fearful to me."

"But it can't hurt you," murmured Diamond, "for you're *it.*"

"Then if I'm *it*, and have you in my arms, how can it hurt you?"

"Oh, yes! I see," whispered Diamond. "But it looks so dreadful, and it pushes me about so."

"Yes, it does, my dear. That is what it was sent for."[14]

Spread the word: This is God's plan; this is God's perspective on the hard stuff. Get with the program. Ask for resurrection power. Don't wait. Ask now. It's your Gift. It's from your Father.

> Now to Him Who is able to do immeasurably more than all we ask or imagine, according to His power that is at work within us, to Him be glory in the church and in Christ Jesus throughout all generations, for ever and ever! Amen.[15]

Thank You, Father. My heart is changed. My mind is renewed. One day at a time.

*   *   *   *

My heart was dramatically changed one summer day in a little plane flying from Boston to Nantucket. I was going to visit my grandchildren, the happy surfing, crabbing, sailing, blue-eyed blonds getting brown and beautiful and salty on the unforgettable northeastern island in the Atlantic Ocean.

I had my old and scruffy Bible in my lap and was reading Acts 3, the chapter we would study in our Monday night Bible study in Chicago the next week. The last verse jumped out at me.

> When God raised up his servant [Jesus], he sent him first to you to bless you by turning each of you from your wicked ways.

I read the verse again. "When God raised up his servant, he sent him first to you to bless you by turning each of you from your wicked ways." God sent Jesus to bless me, and that blessing turned me from my wicked ways! I wondered if I had ever read that verse before. God's blessing is what turns me from my ways to His way.

I had never thought about what saying "God bless you" really meant. If this verse is true, and of course it is, the blessing of God is *very* powerful. I thought I should walk down Michigan Avenue in Chicago and bless everyone I passed. I could say it under my breath; I could bless people and be part of God's plan to turn them from their way to His way.

Then I thought, *I could bless Anne!* I had never "blessed" her in her lesbian relationship because I had a hard stubborn heart. I had never blessed her, because I thought, in my "Christian" lingo, that blessing her would be the same as agreeing with her. I didn't agree with her position, but I loved her and longed to have a relationship with her. It was so hard. Most of the time I didn't know what to do or say.

I thought of all the times I wished I had blessed her: The first time she and Ellen came to Chicago and we had dinner together; I felt so awkward and helpless and cold-hearted and scared. The time I visited them in their gorgeous *Architectural Digest* designer home and they invited some other girlfriends to come to their pool and swim naked. The time we played badminton on their lawn and I beat Ellen (at least that's the way I remember it!). The time we had a really difficult political discussion in their kitchen about gay preachers and gay marriages. I felt awful. I really didn't know what to do.

But now I knew at least one thing I could do. I could confess my sin. And I could bless her. So in that little plane, with my Bible on my lap, I confessed my hard heart and I blessed her, and I blessed her friends.

And as God would have it, that was the weekend she ended her lesbian relationship.

But wait a minute. Sometimes I hesitate to tell that story because it sounds like "ooga booga," poof! I sent up a magic blessing and they broke up. But please appreciate that the real celebration, the real magic or mystery is what happened to my heart. What happened with Anne is another matter. I don't try to explain that. I can only tell my story. It's my heart that was changed so that I could finally bless her.

I believe that the Bible is a book of what God is *doing*, what is happening, not just what God *did*, or what happened hundreds of years ago. God did not speak in Bible times and then go mute! He is speaking things into existence all the time.

The blessing was not intended only for the passersby or the onlookers in Jerusalem 2,000 years ago. It works *now*. God is blessing people today, through you and me, with the same result of turning us from our ways to His way. It's predictable and hopeful. I learn what to expect today by reading what God did yesterday. It's very scientific, actually. If a scientist performs an experiment over and over and gets the same result each time, she can expect that the same thing can and will happen each and every other time.

When I got home from my sun-and-surf vacation, I got out my Greek lexicon to study the word "blessing." Here's what I read: to bless is to ask God to interfere, to take action in one's life, to bring them to the desired relationship with Himself so that they are truly blessed and fully satisfied. After reading that, I thought I should bless everyone all the time! Read it again. To bless is to ask God to interfere, to take action in one's life, to bring them to the desired relationship with Himself . . . Do you get how powerful this is?

Pass along the blessing. Bless everyone!

Jacob and Esau—twin brothers whose story is told in the book of Genesis in the Old Testament—got it. Jacob lied to his father in order to get the blessing intended for Esau, the firstborn, because he knew that the blessing releases God's power to change the character and destiny of the one being blessed. *Wow!*

This blessing became a small obsession for me with my Monday night group. I wanted us to learn to bless each other, not with a casual "Bless you," or "God bless," but with a knowing, informed, passionate, intentional *"BLESS* YOU!" We committed to blessing those who annoyed us in traffic, colleagues who frustrated us at work, friends and family who hurt us at home. When we were together, we collected a $1 fine if someone started to gossip or criticize anyone else. "Bless them!" we would shout. "You owe me a dollar!" was the next holler, with a big laugh and an outstretched hand. Linda loved the idea and was the most diligent, so she always ended up with the biggest stash of dollar bills. She gave it back when she treated everyone to Starbucks. Another blessing!

God bless you. God bless me.

*   *   *   *

When I think of You and the coming days
When the kingdoms fall and Your reign begins
Everything in me longs to see the day
To sing the never ending song

My God is King of all the earth
My God is King forevermore
The nations come to worship Him
My God is King forevermore

Bright and Morning Star—Hope of all the earth
You will shine Your light like the rising sun
There will be no end to Your kingdom's rule
All creation sings the everlasting song

My God is King of all the earth
My God is King forevermore
The nations come to worship Him
My God is King forevermore.[16]

CHAPTER ELEVEN

Empathy

June 2005

"I never knew how much I hurt my mother until I heard your speech last night," the tall, dark-haired young man confesses to me when he finds me in the dining hall at the Exodus conference in North Carolina.[1] He puts his backpack on an empty chair and sits down beside me. "I guess maybe I should talk to her; what do you think?"

"Well, I know I appreciated every conversation that Anne and I had. Your mom will probably gobble up anything you have to say to her. Trust your gut!" I smile, thinking about how that conversation could be so healing for both of them.

At another conference, a tearful, middle-aged man edges down beside me in the front row of the auditorium and says, "I never knew how much I hurt my wife until I heard your speech tonight." He hangs his head and weeps.

This conversation and confession is harder for me. I had never heard those words from my husband about his double life with homosexuality, and it's hard to keep forgiving him, even now. This emotional exchange with the guilty, sad-eyed man brings up a lot of ambivalence for me. Maybe I could take out all my old hurt and anger on this poor unsuspecting spouse in the seat next to me.

"What did you *think?*" I wanted to jab at him. "How could you be so stupid?! What did you think she would feel when she found out?! Jerk!" (Sorry, I'm still a work in progress; but don't worry, I didn't say it.)

"How would it be for you to talk to her about your feelings and your new insight?" I said. *That's better.* I take a deep breath. If the Holy Spirit can convince this man of the pain resulting from his hurtful, adulterous choices and turn him around, and forgive him, then I can too. I peel off and discard one more layer of my anger toward my husband.

Isn't that how God works? I think I'm helping someone, and instead I probably get more of what I need than he does. It's a clear sign that I'm in the right kingdom.

*   *   *   *

"I want to be known as a guy who loves gays." This was how Pat Boone began his speech at the annual N.A.R.T.H. conference in Marina del Rey, California, in November 2005. (N.A.R.T.H. is the National Association for Research and Therapy of Homosexuality.)

Great comment! I thought.

I want to be like Pat Boone—*I* want to be known as a *gal* who loves gays. In this phase of "ministry" in my life, it's a very important "love," a very important identity. I want to be known as a person who respects and loves a group of people who have felt hated by Christians and reject-ed by the Church. It's a group with whom I have maintained a great dis-tance in the past.

I discovered that Pat has been a long-time supporter of N.A.R.T.H. "I'm blessed to be able to use any platform I have to help break down the barriers between the Church and the gay community," Pat said. He puts his money where his mouth is.

Then it is my turn to speak. I had been asked to share my story to this wonderful group of donors and dinner guests gathered that cool evening on the porch of the Marriott Inn. "Well," I begin, "I'm with Pat. I want to be known as a *gal* who loves gays!" (If you've been with me on my journey through this book, you know that's a major breakthrough for me.)

"I thought I was finished with homosexuality when my daughter Anne got married—to a great guy—in September 2001," I said. "I was pos-itive that I had polished that part of my life—except for each time I heard the word 'homosexual' and felt a little sting."

I told them about Queen Esther, my beloved role-model queen—not yet a queen at this point in her story, but rather an innocent young Jewish girl who had been carried into exile from Jerusalem to the citadel of Susa to become a candidate as King Xerxes' new queen. I reminded them, "Even as a queen, Esther did not reveal her nationality and family background to her new companions at the palace." Many in the dining room this night knew about Queen Esther because of their annual Jewish celebration, Purim, in her honor. I was preaching to the choir, so to speak.

I continued, "My hunch is that Esther thought she was finished with Judaism when she came to this foreign land and this fancy palace. In the same way that I thought I had run the race to the finish line for homosexuality, I can imagine that Esther believed that she had completed the suffering that went along with being a Jew. She was safe here. She was home free. No one needed to know her true identity, her past experiences. Yeah, me too. But it's in our blood now; it's our experience now. We can't escape!

"However, when the prime minister—wicked, jealous Haman—sent out a decree that the Jews in the land were to be killed, her Uncle Mordecai challenged Esther, 'The Jews will be saved somehow, but who knows but that *you* have come to the kingdom for such a time as this.'[2]

"She was, you might say, in the right place at the right time. Or maybe not. But it's not because she was a Jew that she was able to save her people from annihilation. There's more to the story than that. Yes, she was a Jew; so her heart was turned toward her people. But there were probably other Jewish girls in the palace who had obtained some favor with the king and who loved their Jewish heritage.

"What is special about Esther is that she had a commitment; more than that, she had a burning passion to see her people delivered from the cruel hands of Haman. She would do whatever it took to save her people. 'If I perish, I perish,' she told Mordecai."

When I recounted this at the conference, I looked straight at Arthur and Jane Goldberg, my engaging dinner partners, and praised Queen Esther. "You know, Arthur, you wouldn't even be here if it weren't for Queen Esther!" I said. He smiled and threw a kiss into the air for his brave queen. (Arthur's rabbi friend suggested to me later that perhaps deliverance *could* have come some other way, but Esther was afforded the opportunity to save her people, and she was a willing servant.)

"I'm probably not quite there—'If I perish, I perish'; but when my children express concern for my safety and/or my reputation as I travel around the country speaking with families and church congregations about the issue of homosexuality, I figure, 'Yes, if I perish, I perish'. I can't turn back now. I have clearly come to the kingdom for such a time as this.

"Please understand me; I am not talking about *saving* the homosexuals. Oh, that's part of it, if some of them need saving. But I'm talking about saving the Church—the ones who are the hypocritical, forked-tongue, double-minded, hard-hearted 'saints' who live in the 'us' versus 'them' world; the ones who might watch television and movies about gays but certainly never speak to one; the self-righteous ones who smugly 'love the sinner but hate the sin' and separate themselves from both. Or even the sad and confused and caring ones who have a blessing locked up inside of them and are just waiting to hear that it's okay to bless, to extend grace and empathy to everyone, yes, even to your gay neighbor—*especially* to your gay neighbor.

"Not that I'm Queen Esther, but I believe that I have come to the kingdom of homosexuality for such a time as this. This is my opportunity to take what God has been working into me over the course of many years—some respect, some empathy, some understanding, some love—and be part of God's plan to serve His people, maybe even to help save some of them like Queen Esther did, and surely to save and rescue me.

"Esther called together her handmaidens in order to get support and prayer. What a great scene! The gorgeous girls of the harem are on their dainty knees, praying for wisdom and discernment and a Holy Spirit strategy for their faithful queen.

"This is why we come to conferences such as N.A.R.T.H. They are so important. We come together to get support. We pray for wisdom and discernment. We strategize together in order to serve and to save God's people. It's very clear that we all have come to the Kingdom for such a time as this."

*   *   *   *

The morning after the dinner, I'm scheduled to teach a workshop for spouses, parents and siblings of family members who are in a same-sex relationship. The crowd developed into a melting pot of psychiatrists, physicians, parents, siblings, pastoral counselors and young singles who are clients of some of the clinicians. It is a bittersweet time for families who are in the throes of managing a whole range of emotions after learning from their loved one that she or he is gay. When they come to the workshop, many are sad and depressed, but also hopeful, looking for the encouragement that comes from being together and sharing stories with others.

I go to the room half an hour before the participants are due to arrive—I want to check on the arrangement of the chairs. "Just as I suspected," I mutter to myself. All the chairs and tables are lined up in very formal straight rows facing the front. I get busy. I don't like the chairs in straight rows. I like them arranged in a circle, or semi-circle at best. I like the participants to see each other. I want to lead the group, but I don't want the attention to be on me all the time. I'm the facilitator, not the main attraction. The room is long and narrow, and the chairs are behind long skinny tables as if we're going to eat lunch together. I can't create as much of an informal setting as I would like, but I heave the furniture around so that I'm happy by the time people start coming through the door.

"Please, come sit in the front," I urge the first three women who come through the door. "I don't like to be alone up here!"

It's my way of soothing my nervous tension and creating a comfortable space for myself as well as the participants. "Please tell me your reason for being here," I invite them to disclose.

"We're here with our priest who runs the support group for parents at our parish," Joann explains. "Some of our group have kids who are gay, and I have a sister who is gay."

"Hi, I'm Mary. My son just told me he's gay, and he's spending all of his time with my brother who is gay. I can't even speak to either of them, I'm so mad. What should I do?"

"We're here from the East Coast. We're part of Jonah, the support group within the Jewish community. We come to the conference every year. Thanks for sharing your story with us. It's nice to meet you."

"Our 18-year-old son told us about a year ago that he was gay. We looked everywhere for some help before we found N.A.R.T.H. This is my wife, and this is our 22-year-old son and our 20-year-old daughter. We're here to get any help you can give us."

"Hi, I'm Jake. I'm a client of Dr. Nicolosi. I've heard some of your story, and I wanted to meet you and hear what you have to say."

The room continues to fill up as I greet people. I love groups. I'm energized by the interaction and ideas that flow when people come together. Remember the Olympian runner Eric Liddell, in the movie *Chariots of Fire?* "I feel His pleasure when I run," he explained to his worried sister.

Well, I feel God's pleasure when I work with groups, although now I feel overwhelmed! I'm shaky and a little teary when I begin to tell my story, first about my husband, then about my daughter.

"I wish I had done things differently," I tell the group, "but I didn't know about N.A.R.T.H.!" Everyone laughs and gives a little cheer.

I have about 45 minutes to share my story, do some teaching and answer questions. Because I want to have plenty of time for the group to engage with each other, I hurry through my "tale of woe," mostly wanting them to know that I have had many of the same emotions they feel—anger, sadness, confusion, shame, embarrassment, fear.

I begin by talking about what happened when my husband died of AIDS. "Our *perfect* Christian family—our children were 14, 17, 18 and 26—was a sham; my marriage was a joke. We didn't know anything about AIDS, and we certainly didn't talk about homosexuality, especially in the church.

"Do you remember that line in the movie *The Firm,* when Tom Cruise's character is told by the F.B.I. man, 'Your life, as you know it, is over'? Well, it was the same for us. We had lived in an environment of betrayal, deception, unconfessed sin and addiction. That environment almost destroyed us. From our "perfect" Christian life we fell into some very dark places in our years of silent pain and grief and loss.

"I made most of the worst decisions of my life in those lonely years.

"They were years of resentment and bitterness, mostly targeted toward the homosexual community. They—that whole phantom world I conjured up in my head—had done me wrong! Why didn't God do something?

"Well, God did begin to do something—in me. He stirred up a renewal, a revival, in me. I remembered a Bible verse that my children memorized in the car going back and forth to church on Sunday mornings and Sunday evenings:

> When all kinds of trials and temptations crowd into your life don't resent them as intruders but welcome them as friends. Realize that they come to test your faith and produce in you the quality of endurance.[3]

"Remembering that verse began to give me God's perspective on the difficult events of my life. There was a method in the madness: *test my faith, produce endurance.* I knew that God placed a high premium on endurance and living life well, without fear and anger and hatred.

"We have to know that God has a sense of humor and an uncanny sense of timing. It was while I was working on endurance and healing from my husband's bad news, and my wayward wanderings, that I got the devastating phone call from my daughter. It seemed impossible! How could this happen again? But you know how God is—He always gives us a second chance to get it right.

"As I began to get the information I needed for my spiritual growth and healing, I also began to get the theoretical and psychological information I needed for my emotional growth and understanding.

"This information has changed my life and brought me to a place of greater love and respect for my husband and my daughter, and for the gay community and those who struggle with same-sex attraction. I had finally found some pieces of the puzzle that I had wanted for so long— from scientists and clinicians, as well as from other parents and spouses and pastors and priests.

"I learned the hard way," I tell the group, "through a lot of angry words and isolation. But I'm getting to the other side of that fear and anger.

"I have learned from Melissa Fryrear, at the Love Won Out conferences, that some of the reasons a woman turns to another woman for
love is that she may have misunderstood or misperceived her mother's
love. Or she may have little respect for the role her mother takes in her
marriage and determines to never take that role herself. She may try to
fill the hole of deep emotional hurt and loss with affection and sexual
love with another woman. In the light of that information, her same-sex
attraction makes sense.

"My children had a very difficult childhood shadowed by secrecy
and deception. My 'mother love' was based in discipline and legalism
and making sure that everything looked right. My role as a wife was
unenviable and even tragic. No wonder. My daughter's behavior
made a lot of sense when I listened with an open heart. A psychia-
trist/writer/professor, whose name I don't remember, instructs his
counseling students to offer to their clients this gift of empathy:
You must have had some very good reasons for doing what you did. I needed
to develop that kind of empathy.

"I learned from Dr. Nicolosi that most scientific studies suggest that
there are factors that may contribute to the condition of male homosexuality such as poor communication between parents and child, an emotionally over involved mother who has a strong, dominant personality;
and a quiet, withdrawn, unexpressive or hostile father.

"The son may be temperamentally shy, timid, introverted, artistic
and imaginative. He may have a special, close relationship with his
mother and a guarded, ill-at-ease or antagonistic relationship with his
father, and even with an older brother. He may display some same-sex
attraction as an attempt to 'repair' some childhood emotional hurts and
to restore what is missing.

"Finally, I had been given some answers! This was the information
I longed for. I could finally begin to make some sense out of my husband's choice to run after other men. Dr. Nicolosi's explanation of some
of the conditions that contribute to male homosexuality fits my husband's childhood environment to a 'T.'"

I continue sharing my story, finding tender, teary eyes and sympathetic nods when I search the crowd for support.

"We are in this together as perpetrators of the hurt from both sides—the angry gay and the angry straight—needing to understand how each of us can close the gap and contribute to the healing.

"I learned from Austrian-born Heinz Kohut, founder of the theory of Self Psychology, some psychological theories that answered some other questions I had about women and men who become involved in same-sex relationships. He believes that one's sense of self and well-being is developed within the context of healthy interpersonal relationships—most particularly good parent-child interaction.

"One's primary means for growth and change is facilitated through relationships—all kinds of relationships. The healthy sense of self and well-being evolves through healthy friendship and/or family relationships; low self-esteem and poor sense of self may be the result of other kinds of relationships—unhealthy friendship and/or parent-child interaction that are abusive, critical, demeaning, and so on.

"Thus, a child who is needy and hurting may fall into or even create relationships with others who are broken and fragmented themselves—others who are also trying to restore and reconcile their own early relationships, trying to heal their own old wounds.

"We all yearn for somebody who will serve as a substitute for those who didn't provide the primary nourishment we need. We're looking for empathy—someone who understands that we are hurting. Kohut says that we're looking for attunement—someone who is 'in tune' with us. Thus, two needy, hurting women look for what they missed in their childhood—a mother's warmth and love; and two hurting needy men look for what they missed in their childhood—a father's strong, caring validation of their masculinity.

"He defines three basic relational needs essential for creating a solid sense of self and a healthy emotional structure: twinship, idealization and mirroring. Understanding these three basic needs helped me take inventory of the way I created or didn't create that kind of environment for my children. (It also helped me understand myself a little better as I took stock of *my* childhood.)

"I remember them by the acronym TIM.

- T—the *twinship* need—the need to experience that others are like me; that others can share my ideas, my dreams. It's the sense that I know you are in tune with me—you *get* me.
- I—the *idealizing* need—the need to be connected to a greater ideal, a calming reality; the need to be connected to one who will listen and not go nuts when they hear some 'bad' news.
- M—the *mirroring* need—the need for recognition, acceptance, adoration, delight, joy when you see me.

I am pouring out my heart to the participants who are sitting on the edge of their seats wanting to get help and hope. There's an audible sigh of relief when they hear that there are some "scientific" explanations for a same-sex attraction. It's not that the parents abdicate responsibility or shrug their shoulders, believing there's nothing they can do; but they are able to hear what they might have neglected in the parenting process. I know—I've been in that seat. I'm in tune with them!

Now they want to hear if there's anything they can do to change their situation. Here, then, is the heart of my story: "It's not about trying to change anyone else; it's about changing *my* heart and *my* behavior. This is why I titled this presentation 'It's All About Me'. I am sold-out, no-turning-back passionate about changing *me!*

"These three needs—twinship, idealizing, mirroring—are met through our interpersonal relationships. The needs exist from birth though old age. When we work on getting these primary needs met for ourselves through healthy relationships, and we have gained some sense of our own value or right to life and right to assert ourselves and be happy, we probably will have a healthy sense of self and well-being. We can make decisions out of our wholeness instead of our woundedness. We can express empathy to our loved ones.

"We are able to understand that if these needs are not met, for ourselves as well as our loved ones, we/they may end up feeling hurt, devalued, belittled, criticized, shamed. We/they develop an underlying, simmering hurt and anger that may come out in our behavior as defensiveness, overachievement, withdrawal, depression, and/or addictive behavior to cover the hurt, pain and rejection.

"Sometimes the result is a same-sex attraction and struggle, and/or living homosexually. (Sometimes it's a sad, depressed heterosexual.)

"Okay, that's the theory. What's the practice? I want to give these people some specific tools to take home—to help them on their own journey of personal growth and change and healing.

"Let's start with twinship.

"How does one meet a *twinship* need?" I ask the group.

"You communicate twinship to another through expressing a deep understanding of her situation and how it relates to her past—you acknowledge that you can imagine why she feels this way, thinks this way, acts this way, why she does what she does. Here are some responses that express twinship:

- "You must have had a good reason for _____
  _____."
- "Oh, when I hear what you just told me, I can imagine that you felt hurt and rejected and belittled. You have every right to be angry."
- "You make a lot of sense. I get it."

"You may meet twinship needs by communicating that if you were in her shoes, you could understand why she made the decisions she did. You don't have to agree with her decisions; but after hearing her side of the story, you get it."

Then I take a risk. I think the room is full of believers now, so I put them to the test. (This is what I love the most—getting them to follow my directions, interact with each other and come back totally engaged and connected.)

"I have always wondered what it would have been like to have a good conversation with my husband—one honest, broken adult to another. Or what it would have been like if I could have responded differently when I got Anne's phone call about her and Ellen."

So I ask the group to role-play and to pretend they are in my shoes, in my house, on my phone, listening to Anne.

"And now," I say to them, "partner with your neighbor and one of you take Anne's part and say to your partner the words Anne said to me: 'I've fallen in love with a woman.' And then the other partner takes my part and gives a twinship kind of response like I wish I had given."

I give them an example, wishing that I could have said the words, "Oh, wow. Well, I imagine you have some very good reasons. I hope we can talk soon—" or something like that.

Everyone turns to someone beside him or her. The room fills with giggles and guffaws when I ask the attendees to do this role-playing— "No way!" "He's a priest! I'm a woman. It's not right for either of us!" The two straight male psychiatrists find it a real possibility to fall in love with a woman! The troubled family struggles with the frivolity. It is a quick change of pace from my lecture, so everyone has to get themselves into the right frame of mind before they can do the role-playing I have requested. We agree, after we settle down, that it's harder than you think to meet another's need when we ourselves are needy. It's hard to say, "You must have a very good reason for doing it" when your heart is breaking.

- "TWINSHIP—You acknowledge to the other some of your likenesses. 'I am in tune with you.' 'You must have . . .' 'I can imagine . . .' 'I get it'.

"Let's move on to idealizing. How does one meet an idealizing need?"

"You model the compassionate, understanding, validating and supportive characteristics that will eventually, you hope, become part of the other's healthy sense of self and emotional structure.

"Oh, boy, have I *not* done that! I have yelled into the phone; I have pouted and withheld all compassion and support. I wish I could have been calm and understanding. I wish I could have said

- 'Tell me more.'
- 'I'd like to listen to you. I'm open to hearing what you have to say.'
- 'I care about you and what you're thinking and feeling.'

I ask the group to give a before-and-after idealizing response—something that expresses an immature reaction and then something that sounds supportive and understanding. After a lot of chatter, one voice stands out: "It's easy to give the 'before' reaction," one parent confesses to the group. Everyone is in tune with him.

"IDEALIZING—You are calm, mature, objective, able to be respected and admired, 'cool', able to listen and change and adapt. You model the behavior you hope to receive yourself.

"Next is mirroring. How does one meet a mirroring need?

"You respond to the other's needs—cherishing, valuing the communication, delighting in her. It's as if you are saying

- 'You're adorable.'
- 'I love to talk with you—I value your ideas and opinions.'
- 'My heart jumps with joy when I see you and hear from you.'

"And have I done that? Oh, no! My daughters would say, "'Mom, you have that look!' And they don't mean an affirming look."

"MIRRORING—You delight, you adore, you acknowledge the person's right to life, to abundant life."

I'm out of time. We have a warm, sympathetic discussion, acknowledging that we are works in progress. We thank each other for being there, for caring, crying, melting our hearts in those connecting, comforting moments together.

One last question comes from a woman seated in the very back row, squeezed into a corner: "What do you say to a wife whose heart is broken and who feels utterly hopeless?" I remember Stephanie Goeke's story from Exodus International. Her husband left their marriage for a homosexual season, but she never gave up. She's a wonder. And Mike, her husband, *is* back, fully restored.

"Never give up," I say. "Never stop growing yourself; never stop praying. Never, never, never give up."

I conclude by saying, "You parents (and spouses) don't have to 'therapize' or 'catastrophize' or 'pathologize.' The professionals may do that. But here's what you can do: You can be 'glue.' In Eugene O'Neill's play *Great God Brown,* he writes, 'Man is born broken. He lives by mending. The grace of God is the glue.' I encourage you to pray for glue! And pray that you will be glue, too—full of God's grace.

"Thank you so much. You have been a wonderful group."

I feel His pleasure as we crowd together on the way to the elevator.

✳   ✳   ✳   ✳

I call my friend Jan. "This is the verse for the day for me; listen to this!" We're always ready to hear what the Lord says to each of us from our morning reading and prayer time. It's usually good for both of us.

> Remember how the LORD your God led you all the way in the desert those forty years; to humble you and to test you in order to know what was in your heart, whether or not you would keep his commands.[4]

"Ah, the truth comes out. My life is really in the Word. But does it have to take 40 years?" We laugh about it, both of us hitting a 40-year mark of faith.

"You know that I took a detour from God for a season in those 40 years," I say. "But He surely led me all the way. I have been humbled and tested. And He knows what is in my heart now, and that I'm committed to keeping His commands. Do you think I can say that this verse describes my life?"

She agrees—the Word actually explains my life.

My life is in the Word.

CHAPTER TWELVE

Mercy

The bright yellow poster on the dining hall bulletin board read:

SEXUAL ORIENTATION:
Truth and Love from a Unique Perspective
DR. NANCY HECHE, SPEAKER

As a single parent who experienced the international media rush during her daughter Anne's highly visible lesbian relationship and a widow who survived her husband's shocking diagnosis and subsequent death [the poster said dearth!] of AIDS, after a secret double life, Nancy brings a compassionate and unique focus to the realities of living with both the secret and public aspects of homosexuality in a family. She has a private practice in psychotherapy and specializes in communication and relationship issues with families, couples and singles. Her college courses and seminars are highly valued for their practical approach to some of the sensitive and painful issues of life.

Thursday, October 27, 2005, 7:00 p.m.
UNIVERSITY OF SOUTHERN MAINE
Masterton Hall—Room 113
Sponsored by USM College Republicans

This notice was plastered all over the USM campus in Portland, two weeks before a statewide election in which one of the items on the ballot had to do with including sexual orientation in the list of protected classes in Maine's civil rights laws. What was a nice girl like me doing in a gig like this? I could get crucified, or at least be labeled certifiably insane! I'm from the wrong age group, the wrong sexual orientation, the wrong part of the country, the wrong political party—I would have to beg this group for mercy.

It all started with a phone call from Sandy Williams, pastor of the First Baptist Church of Freeport, Maine. Sandy was a leader during this political campaign to repeal the referendum that pertained to sexual orientation. He initially extended his invitation to me from the Christian Civic League and the Coalition for Marriage. These two groups were interested in defeating the referendum that was being put to the voters on November 8, because it defined sexual orientation as "actual or perceived heterosexuality, homosexuality, bisexuality or gender identity or expression." They believed that "sexual orientation," in this case, was an invented category that contributed to increased gender confusion; and Sandy believed that I could offer a different perspective to the voters from the usual "gay versus straight" agenda.

When I said yes to Sandy, I imagined myself with a group of pastors from the Christian Civic League sitting side by side with educators and students in a friendly setting, nodding in agreement, smiling, wearing outdoorsy conservative jackets and jeans, with conservative haircuts, maybe a little conservative makeup, holding Bibles and notebooks in hand—one mind, one body, one spirit. It would be a slam dunk. I would pretty much give the same speech that I give at the Love Won Out conference sponsored by Focus on the Family. I would tell my story and encourage parents and pastors and congregations to change their own lives before they try to get those in the gay community to change theirs.

I checked my calendar and told Sandy yes. "I'll be happy to speak to your group. I can put a little different twist on relating to the gay community and share how God has changed my heart and behavior around this whole issue of homosexuality."

I assumed that there was a lot of tension around this issue and I could imagine that tempers were on edge. I was ready to stand on my kinder, gentler soapbox to suggest a kinder, gentler way of dealing with the "other side."

Blessed are the merciful, for they shall receive mercy.

The next phone call a few days later caught me off guard. It was Sandy again. "Nancy," he said, "I think we'll have the Campus Republicans at the University of Southern Maine in Portland sponsor the event. Do you think you could share some of your story in this public forum and also speak a little about the referendum?"

Well, I am a registered Republican, and I teach college students; so that part isn't too scary . . . "Okay," I said to Sandy with a laugh. "But this changes things, you know. I can't give my usual speech filled with Scripture verses and tears. By the way, is this a friendly group—these College Republicans—and will there be hecklers and . . . and . . . and . . . ?"

Suddenly the event had become a political rally! From personal experiences when my father ran political campaigns decades ago, and as recently as the past national presidential election and every local election in Chicago, I knew that political campaigns are far from kind and gentle. I wondered, *Have I come to the kingdom for such a time as this? Seriously, am I "called" to do this?*

Go into all the world and . . . whatever!

"I don't think I can speak very intelligently about the political issue," I confided to Sandy. But I agreed to speak to the unexpected and unsuspecting campus crowd. When I hung up the phone, I took a deep breath and began to talk myself into it—"I teach college kids; I *love* college kids! I'm creative." I'll have to be very creative and very cool to keep their attention. That's the big challenge. I have to earn the right to be heard—I'm a stranger, a Midwesterner, a grandmother to kids their age, besides all the other ways I'm wrong for this group. Why would they listen to me for a minute? I haven't a clue!

I called my granddaughter Elise, a senior at the University of Michigan, and asked for help.

"Well," Elise said, "on most campuses, the 'Dems' outlive the Republicans. It could be a tough crowd. Don't make it into an 'us and them' situation. Just show them that you care."

She saved my life. (She's brilliant.)

Remembering the old adage "Know your enemies," I called Jason Lavoie, chairman of the College Republicans, and got him on his cell phone between classes. "Can you tell me what you expect next week—who you think will show up?" I asked him. I was freaking out a bit, picturing a crowd of either 2 or 2,000.

"There will be a real diverse mix of kids," Jason said, "most of them on the NO side of this issue as opposed to our YES. They're a pretty intense group, deeply invested in their resistance. Some might be a little hostile—they might stage a demonstration outside the lecture hall. And, oh, some of the kids will be writing papers on your speech to fulfill an assignment from a professor. Any more questions? Gotta run. Call me later."

It was a whole new ballgame.

Here's how I played it: I was going to need a gadget play, like the Pittsburgh Steelers football team uses to surprise their opponents. I had to get the audience hooked when they came in the door, and I had to do something they probably hadn't seen before.

I went to the lecture hall early and hung a clothesline from one end of the whiteboard to the other. Then I folded five large tent cards over the rope and spread them out—two on the far left, one in the middle and two on the far right. The words printed on the two cards on the left-hand side were FEAR and ANGER. The middle card had a big red arrow that pointed to the cards on the right. The words printed on the two cards on the right-hand side of the whiteboard were RESPECT and LOVE.

The clothesline represented the timeline of my life during the previous 25 years around the issue of homosexuality. (Most of the audience probably hadn't even seen their twenty-fifth birthday!) The cards represented my emotions and the change of direction in my life during that period of time. I created the cards with the hope that they would be a pretty effective visual that I could refer to several times in my 45 to 50 minutes standing in front of them.

Everything was ready. The press was there, and I had given a five-minute TV interview earlier in the day. We, the Republicans and the Baptists, had prayed behind closed doors. Even so, "It had all the makings of a heated political fight," was how reporter Mark Peters from the *Portland Press Herald* began his front-page news story the day after the event.

I was nervous as I waited for the audience to arrive, feeling as wary and worried as the campus crowd. I had intended to change from my jean jacket and travel clothes into skirt and boots and other jacket, and freshen my makeup; but in the end, I was happy that I hadn't had time. I needed to be as casual and approachable as possible. My new Calvin Klein jacket would have put me a million miles away from these kids. I took Elise's advice not to make it an "us and them" situation. I wasn't pretending that I could be 20 again, or bisexual or multipierced, or a Democrat; but I wanted to break down some barriers in any way that I could. I pretended that my jean jacket could be one of them.

I guessed that greeting them at the door was another.

"Hi, I'm Nancy. Thanks for coming. What's your name?"

I feel God's pleasure when I connect with these kids now—in a serendipity kind of way. Gail, Donnie, Brant, Allyson—pierced and painted and belligerent. They shake my hand, force a smile and show me their big bright red NO button on their way to find a seat. I welcome everyone as they come in single file. They go past the podium and up the stairs of the tiered lecture hall. The 20 or so nondescript YES people fade away as the 70 to 80 multicolored students fill the hall with their banners and posters and passion. They had huddled outside the building, plotting and planning, keeping those of us on the inside wondering if they were going to come inside or not; and if so, when and how? Peters wrote in his newspaper article, "An organizer reminded them beforehand to be respectful." (Thank you.)

Now I look up at the crowd settled in, row upon row, all the way to the top row 20 feet or so above me. (Remember Barbra Streisand in the role of a college professor as she lectured students in the movie *The Mirror Has Two Faces*? This lecture hall was a smaller version of that one.) The tiers allow me to see each inquisitive face, each NO button, each six-foot banner draped over the backboard in front of the desks: VOTE NO ON TUESDAY. VOTE NO FOR DISCRIMINATION.

I jump right into the deep end, already aware that I'm probably in over my head. They'll either love me or hate me. But I really want them to love me! They're looking right at me; there's no turning back.

"Hi, I'm Nancy Heche. Thanks so much for being here.

"I'm inviting you to come along on part of my journey through my experience with the issue of homosexuality. You can probably guess what it has been like for me by seeing these signs on the clothesline behind me.

"First, I'll explain what this clothesline is all about: The clothesline represents some of the last 25 years of my life, starting about the time the fear and anger began. I hope you'll hear the two Aha! moments that got me moving from the fear and anger side of my life into the respect and love side. I call it my 'extreme makeover'!

"I'll be asking for your participation along this journey, and if you have any questions, write them down and we'll discuss them at the end.

"Because I'm trained in psychotherapy, and I love working with groups, this will be somewhat like a large group therapy session. How does that sound?" They probably weren't sure what I meant by that, and I wasn't sure how it would work, but I knew I didn't want to do all the talking. I love the interaction and synergy of a diverse group sharing their thoughts and feelings together; so I was going to give it a whirl.

"Here are the ground rules for my groups:

1. Please respond when I invite you to participate.
2. One person talks at a time. Please, if you want to add anything or comment along the way, just let me know. I want to hear what you have to say. If it can wait, write it down and we'll discuss it later.
3. I'm sure I would like you if we had a chance to get to know each other, and I'm assuming you would like me, even if we don't agree!

And what's said here, stays here.

"Oh no, that's in Vegas." (They laugh, sort of, and I relax a little.)

I begin my story with the scene in the New York hospital in 1983, when I heard the words from the doctor, "Hasn't anyone told you, Mrs. Heche? Your husband is dying . . . of AIDS." That one shocking statement outed my husband's double life and betrayed a 25-year-old secret. I had no clue! How could I?!

"We had been married 25 years. We were living our perfect Christian family life—teaching Sunday School and Bible studies, directing the church choir, going to church Sunday morning, Sunday evening, Wednesday evening—a perfect, beautiful Christian family, so people said, and so I thought."

I stop telling my story. "This is where the group therapy session begins. Here are the directions: Turn to your neighbor and say something like this: 'After hearing what she just told us, I can imagine that she felt (fill in the blank).' If you need any hints, look at the clothesline.

"Then write down your own reaction—how you felt or what you thought in the moment—not the past, but right here, right now. Say, 'After hearing what she just told us, I felt (fill in the blank).' Your first response is about me—how you think I might have felt; your second response is about you—how you felt.

"This is the therapy part—you try to put yourself in another's shoes—in my shoes tonight—and imagine how I felt. After that, you record your own feelings: 'After hearing what she said, I felt _____.' The first response represents the skill of empathy—understanding how I felt from my perspective. The second response represents the skill of self-awareness—understanding how you felt, what's going on with you. Okay, let's try it."

Instant talking. But it doesn't really matter what they say to each other. My goal is to get them on my side just a tiny bit—to get them to feel for a moment what I felt, or at least to imagine what I might have felt, and then to be able to acknowledge their own feelings. I'm trying to minimize the "us versus them" mentality and wanting each group to have some understanding and mercy for the other. (If we had more time, we would have had an open discussion, using their comments.)

"Okay. Thanks. I'll go on to the next part of my story.

"In 1997, 14 years after my husband died from AIDS, I answered the phone and heard these words from my youngest daughter: 'Hi, Mom, it's Anne. I'm calling to tell you that I've fallen in love . . . with a woman. It just happened—last week at the Oscars. But it's real. It's wonderful. And I wanted to tell you right away because it's going to be very public. I know this is probably a real surprise for you, Mom. Well, I can't talk

now, but I'll call you in a few days to tell you more. Bye, Mom. I love you.'
Once again, I had no clue. How could I? She had dated some pretty interesting men until now.

"Your turn again," I say to the students. "Please turn to your neighbor and say something like this: 'After hearing what she just told us, I can imagine that she felt (fill in the blank).'

"Then write down your own reaction—how you felt or what you thought in the moment. Say, 'After hearing what she just told us, I felt (fill in the blank)'. The first time you respond, it's your comment about me—how you think I might have felt; the second time, it's about you, how you felt."

After a few moments of their interaction with each other, I tell them, "These two events are etched on my heart forever. Many of you probably also remember when you heard from a sister or brother, a friend or a parent the words that changed your life forever—'I'm gay.' Or you remember the first time you said out loud, 'I'm gay.' With either scenario, you wonder

What do I say?
What do I do?
How do I act?
Does everyone know?
Is this my fault? Was I born this way?
Why is this happening to me?

"However, the two events—with my husband and then my daughter—served to expose some of the dark places of fear and anger in my heart and also were the catalyst for the change in my heart.

"I wish I had done things differently, especially when my husband died; but I didn't know where to turn for help. And besides, I thought, *I don't need help, he's the one who needs help; I'm fine!* Also, I didn't want to talk about it anyway—I chose to keep the secret.

"For seven years I kept the secret. I didn't tell anyone that my husband died of AIDS. We said he had died of cancer. On the outside, we tried to act as if nothing happened. *Act as if nothing had happened?* Almost overnight I went from being a Bible-teaching, hard-core disciple to a false-faced phony defector.

"On the inside, I was furious. How could he do this to me? To us? My children said we can't believe anything he ever said. I had lost my past as well as my future. I was hurt and angry and afraid. I was humiliated and embarrassed. What was *wrong* with me anyway? How could I be *so* stupid! And I was baffled—what happened to our marriage? I called into question everything I believed or knew to be right. Our perfect Christian family was a sham. My marriage was a joke.

"'How could you not know?' people asked me. Even my children said, 'Mom, how could you not know?'

"Well, 23 years ago, most of us didn't know much about AIDS, and we certainly didn't talk about homosexuality, especially in the church. How could I not know? Honestly, it never entered my mind.

"It's not hard to imagine that my children and I lost our innocence and got hugely sidetracked from our perfect life.

"Our children were 14, 17, 18 and 26.

"Our lives would never be the same.

"We had lived in an environment of betrayal and deception. That environment almost destroyed us. From our perfect Christian life, we fell into some very dark places in our years of silent pain and grief and loss.

"They were years of resentment and bitterness for me, mostly targeted toward the homosexual community—'*They,*' a whole phantom world I made up in my mind, had done me wrong!

"I carried a big card in my hard heart and it had 'homosexual' scrawled on it. Every time I thought about my husband or my daughter, I took out my big card and waved my ugly sign, full of fear and anger, resentment and bitterness.

"So how did I get from there to here?" I turn and look behind me at the cards with the words FEAR and ANGER scrawled on them and then move the card with the big arrow along the clothesline toward the cards with the words RESPECT and LOVE.

"I had been a woman of strong faith, and I began to get hungry for that connection with God again. I wanted to try to figure out how I could move out of fear and anger to respect and love. From my past, I remembered a phrase, a verse from the Bible, that reads, 'When all kinds of trials and tribulations crowd into your life, realize that they come to test your faith and produce in you the quality of endurance.'[1]

"My first big Aha! was a realization that there was a bigger picture, a design, a plan and a purpose that included the difficult events of my life. There was a method to the madness—*test my faith, produce endurance*. I knew that God placed a high premium on endurance, on moving through life well, and showing a life that manifests love and respect, authenticity and mercy. Knowing that there was a design, a plan, a purpose for my life was the first big Aha!

"The next Aha! came when I realized that I could choose what kind of person I would be: I could either live my life in fear and anger for the way homosexuality had come into my life, or I could choose to live in a way that manifests love and respect to others." I slid the arrow all the way to the far right end of the clothesline, close to the two cards that read LOVE and RESPECT. "The fact that I could choose in which emotional arena I would live my life was the second big Aha!

"So I'm in a good place, right?

"Well, I have a setback. When I received the devastating phone call from my daughter, I had been growing and learning and changing." I pointed to the clothesline to remember how far I had moved. "I was moving right along, recovering from the repercussions of my husband's death from AIDS. But this was a stunning blow. It seemed like the scab of a very deep wound had been ripped off. I couldn't believe it. Test my faith? Produce endurance? *Isn't this going a little too far?*

"This phone call, at this point in my life, made no sense at all. This, now this *really* never entered my mind. It seemed impossible. How could this happen again? I confess—I slipped backwards." I move the arrow back to the left, to the FEAR and ANGER side of the clothesline.

"But I know I really can't go back. Remember my two Aha! moments? Number one Aha! was that there's a bigger picture and a bigger purpose for my life. Number two Aha! was that I can choose how I will live my life. I can't, I won't undo my extreme makeover—all that has been changed and healed.

"I'll tell you what happened. I say, 'It's all about me,' because I discovered that my journey is not about changing my daughter—or changing anyone else. It's about changing ME!" I move the arrow back toward the cards on the right, closer to LOVE and RESPECT.

"I began to meet some great people (who also happened to be homosexuals!) I learned to respect and love them the same way I would respect and love anyone else. God was teaching me about love, about loving my husband and daughter and loving that phantom world I had made up in my mind.

"I began to realize that when I speak, people will plug their ears and say 'lalalalala' if I don't have love.

"I can get my academic degrees and know a little bit about a lot of things, but they mean nothing without love.

"I can even win the lottery and give it all away, but it means nothing without love.

"It's not about how much I say or how much I know or how much I do—it's about how much I love." I move the arrow a little bit more to the right.

" 'We are invited, drawn into the heart of God, invited to look at people and the world through the eyes of God, full of love.' I was being drawn into this kind of love, drawn into the heart of God where I could be changed and healed.

"Be like the all-loving, all-giving, all-forgiving, everything-I-have-is-yours kind of person who does not measure out love to others according to how they act or what they believe." I move the card even closer to the right-hand side.

"Maybe you can see now why I say, IT'S ALL ABOUT ME. I discovered that this journey isn't about me getting my daughter—or anyone else—to change. It's about changing me.

"So, to summarize, how did I get from fear and anger to respect and love?

"First, it took seeing the big picture—seeing that there must be more to my life than fear and anger around the issue of homosexuality.

"And second, it took choosing to move away from fear and anger, choosing to connect with others and to move toward love and respect. It was an *extreme makeover!*

"Now the group session is open for questions and comments. Let's go back to one person speaking at a time."

Lots of hands went up. I had no idea what to expect, but here's what happened: Amanda, with a button and a banner, shot up her hand and asked me where I stood on the political issue, pretty much ignoring my story.

"Thanks for your question. Really, though, I'm not here to talk politics," I said. "I'm just sharing my story. Sorry."

"But that's why we came here," Amanda retorted angrily, "to hear your position on this referendum." Because she was the only one who had not looked me in the eye when she walked through the door, I really wanted to connect with her. But I wasn't going to be able to give her an answer that would satisfy her. I felt like a failure.

"Nancy," someone called out. I looked up a couple of rows behind Amanda. One of her friends, Rick, was waving his arm and calling my name. "Nancy!" he shouted. Everyone laughed and turned to him. He was about seven feet tall and stood out in the crowd. He had given me a big smile when we shook hands at the door, and I was eager to hear what he had to say.

"You know, I'm a dyed-in-the-wool Mainer, lived here all my life, going to school here now. If you, an outsider, from the Midwest, had taken a stand on this issue, I wouldn't have much respect for you. No offense, but what would you know about it anyway? So, thanks for your honesty." He gave me a big grin and then looked over at Amanda.

"Thanks, Rick," I said. *Saved by the friendly giant.* "Next question or comment?"

Jack, sitting in the front row, said, "What's your stand on homosexuality?" I knew he had come as part of the YES group, and I wished he hadn't asked *the* question. I had been trying hard to lean toward connection—no "us" and "them," Elise had advised.

"I'm not going to answer that question right now," I replied. "You all probably have a pretty good idea of what I believe about homosexuality; but I confess, I'm a people pleaser. I want you to like me; and so I'm going to wait until we've had some more group discussion and interaction before I answer that question. Thanks. Who's next?"

There, I had said it—I wanted them to like me! And I decided to be totally honest so that if they had any ideas about accusing me of hedging or avoiding, I would have already admitted it.

"What is your goal for being here then?" This question came from another girl high up in the last row. When I started to speak, I felt tears spurting into my eyes and pain rushing to my throat. This was not a good sign, and it didn't seem like a very cool thing to do, to get teary amidst this tough crowd. But I've learned to value tears and to never begrudge them, so I choked a little, laughed a little and then told them one of my theories about "group."

"Here's my theory about 'group' and tears: It's never a really successful group meeting until somebody cries," I said, "so I guess I'll be the first here tonight."

Then I told them my goal for being there—a spontaneous heartfelt confession: "I would like for you to see one person, at least one person, who respects and loves you. You probably don't agree with me on a lot of things, and vice versa, but I respect you and love you and really appreciate your being here to give us a chance to do that with, and for, each other.

"I've been guilty of dishing out some of the disrespect and disdain that you have received at the hands of those who disagree with you. I choose differently now. And I thank you for showing me mercy and giving me your respect."

There were more questions and comments before the meeting broke up—some who wanted to campaign and some who wanted to rant and rave a little. One woman, way over on the far left (literally and logistically), called out, "Do you believe in discrimination?"

"Of course not," I said, knowing that I might shoot myself in the foot with the YES crowd but gain some ground with the NOs. When a cheer went up from the NOs, I wondered how the YESes would react. It was a trick question, but the only direct answer to such a direct question was no. I didn't want to do any fancy footwork or political double-talk; and by now, I knew how to move the discussion right along so we didn't get stuck here.

One NO person got entangled with a YES person, but we got through that too. The NOs and the YESes even talked to each other when the group discussion ended.

I *love* this group! I feel His pleasure tonight. It's a gift of mercy. As my therapist used to say, "Mercy is always flowing."

*   *   *   *

My dictionary says that mercy is kindness in excess of what might be expected. In the spiritual realm, I get mercy from God so that I don't have to feel miserable about my sin all the time or fear that He's going to zap me out of the blue in order to remind me that I have sinned in the past and will continue to sin. He treats me kindly and compassionately in spite of my sin, in excess of what might be expected or deserved. I've been given so much mercy; much is now required of me.

And I get mercy in the natural realm also. Tonight those kids in the college lecture hall extended so much mercy to me. They didn't remind me of my hateful past. They didn't presume that my past behavior was the only predictor of present and future behavior, as if I were still hateful and angry. They took me at my word. They treated me kindly and compassionately, in spite of my sins, in excess of what I expected or deserved. Mercy is always flowing.

I am not required to remind this group of any sins I might suspect they are committing or to threaten them with some future gloom or doom that may or may not zap them out of the blue. I remember the words of a song we sing at my church—"and on that cross where Jesus died the wrath of God was satisfied." I thought, *If God's wrath has been satisfied, so has mine. I'm not going to feel and act angry any longer. I am called, invited, required to be merciful, to treat them kindly and compassionately, in excess of what might be expected or deserved!*

Blessed are the merciful, for they shall receive mercy.

Go into all the world and . . . whatever! This is the world I want to go into—that I am called to. This is the world that demands the best from me—that requires mercy and love and respect from the depths of my transformed heart.

Brant, who came up to me with tears in her/his eyes (I honestly don't know if she was a girl or guy), said, "You touched my heart." Wow! More tears!

Martin looked so sad when he said, "My mother hates me, and her church hates me. They pray for me all the time. My mom just doesn't understand me. What can I do?" He was begging for help.

I cringe. I've been that mother; I've joined that church. But Martin seems to have already forgiven me for my past fear and anger. I guess he took me at my word and believed that I could answer from the love and respect side of my life. (I am given so much more than I deserve.)

"Pray for your mom, Martin," I say, "and pray for your church. Now that you have received love and respect and mercy, pass it on."

Carla told me that she was the head of a Wiccan (the realm of witch-craft), which jarred me a little, and that she appreciated the chance to hear me. "What's your relationship with Anne these days?" She asked the question that usually comes up.

"It's family business," I tell her. "I keep it private. Thanks for being here." *(Really, thanks very much for being here! Bless her, God.)*

Jo (or Joe) talked about her children and how hard it was to be in school and raise kids—the usual problem for an unusual student.

Amanda, who seemed to want to heckle me on the political issue, waited until the room was almost empty. She walked down the steps, came right up and looked me in the eye, and said, "I wanted to tell you that I could imagine that it was very hard for you when Anne got together with Ellen."

*   *   *   *

Sometimes the telling—and the hearing—creates a connection that comforts us, that connects us. We are not alone. We stand together and release our broken hearts. We heal, word by word, hand in hand, friend to friend.

More Truth Comes Out

I wish my story were like Elizabeth's. Hers, yet unfinished, is already remarkable. Just about two years ago, her husband left her to live with his gay boyfriend—his "dude," as her sons call him. (Sometimes you need a little humor to soften the blow.) Elizabeth tells me by e-mail that she still has her days, but she isn't just surviving, she's thriving!

I met Elizabeth at my first Love Won Out conference (a national conference ministry that offers support for friends and families around the issue of their loved ones' homosexuality), a few weeks after her husband had left her. She was still reeling from the separation but grateful for all the information and support she received at the conference. We sat together in the front row and listened and nodded and cried together. Everything we heard helped us to make sense of the bombshells that had exploded in our lives because of our husbands—my bombshell 25 years ago; hers just 6 weeks before this conference we were attending.

Fast forward to today. Elizabeth does not live with a Pollyanna mind-set; she is not wearing rose-tinted glasses or living a "let's pretend" fairy tale. She doesn't hide her sadness or anger or incredulity about her husband of several decades having an affair with another man. But neither does she stay in those painful emotions. She's remarkable!

I have often wondered what decision I would have made about including my gay husband in our family affairs if he were alive. (Sometimes I've actually been grateful that he was dead and I didn't have to worry about it.) Elizabeth had to face that dilemma—here's how she handled it. Her husband asked to be included in a family celebration. She debated a long time before inviting him. During a telephone conversation with me, we wrestled with the hard questions. "Are we supposed to act like one big happy family—it's so odd. The whole world seems upside down. Where do I sit? What do we talk about? Can I really look him in the eye when I speak to him? Do we just ignore the elephant in the middle of the room?"

Well, Elizabeth did invite her husband to the celebration. Her children gave her their okay. And it worked out. From my perspective, that is remarkable! Elizabeth is my hero. She has helped me to grow and heal, 25 years after the fact.

Friends and Their Families

Judy: A Mother's Story About Her Son's Estrangement

My middle son is adopted. We brought him home from the hospital when he was nine days old.

Two months before his graduation from high school, he went to a rehearsal for his senior musical. He was long overdue returning home. Consequently, I was waiting in the living room for his return.

When at last he came home, he sat down in a chair opposite me. I was angry and said, "What's going on? Are you and your girlfriend having sex?" (My worst fear!)

He just looked at me with a very cynical look and said, "You have *no* clue!"

"Then *give* me a clue," I said. "What's going on?"

After a few minutes of just looking at me, he said, "For the past four years I've been living a homosexual lifestyle."

I couldn't speak for several moments. While my husband was peacefully sleeping just a room away, I was having my life turned upside down. I didn't understand how this could be happening in our son's life and our home. I tried to reason with him, but he was very antagonistic and got up and headed for the door to leave.

He announced that he was going to his best friend's sister's house. She had told him that he could stay there if things didn't go well here tonight.

"You're not going anywhere until your father knows what's going on," I said. "Stay right here until I get him!" I woke up my husband and quickly told him what was happening. When he came into the living room, he said to our son, "Get out of here, and don't come back until you've got your life straightened out."

"Think what you're saying!" I shouted.

My husband just continued to look at our son and then calmly said, "Well, that's what I'd like to say, but you're my son and will *always* be my son. Since I can't agree with what you're doing with your life, can we sit down and talk about this?"

"No," our son answered, and walked out the door saying that he would be back the next day for his things.

We were in shock and mourning as our son closed the front door. This precious son whom we loved so much had been deceiving us for the past four years. And he was basically throwing in our face that he had accepted as "truth" that he was homosexual, believing total strangers rather than believing us and what the Bible said.

We were also in mourning because we had to face the death of our dreams for him—dreams for college, marriage, children and a maturing adult relationship with him that we could share on a spiritual level. We felt as if we had failed him as parents because we hadn't seen this coming. And we obviously didn't have a relationship with him where he felt he could come to us about what he was feeling.

Fortunately, we have some very good friends that we called immediately. We woke them up, but they came over at once and wept with us for a couple of hours. None of us slept for the rest of that night. We also called our extended family to let them know of our need for prayer, which I had told our son I was going to do because I wanted him covered with prayer.

The next day, I contacted a friend who gave me a phone number for Spatula Ministries—a ministry to families affected by homosexuality. The woman from Spatula Ministries was very comforting and put me in contact with another mother in my area who was in my position but further down the road in dealing with it.

My husband and I had two birth sons, one five years older and another three years younger, who were not facing this issue. We wondered what we did differently with our middle son.

When he arrived the next day to collect his things (which he had been preparing for a time like this), all four of us were waiting to try to talk him out of pursuing this lifestyle any further. We didn't know what organizations were out there to help him, but we were willing to try to find out. Ultimately, he wouldn't listen, and walked out of our home. His best friend and sister got their mom to agree to let our son stay with them, provided he went to school and graduation—which he did just barely—and which we attended, although it was a strained atmosphere.

We maintained contact with him through the years by phone or by e-mail; and he came to some family gatherings. We attended some of his performances and always showed him our unconditional love. But just recently, while visiting him in California, he informed me that because I won't agree that his lifestyle is "normal," he finds it necessary to end further contact with me and is legally changing his last name. We were both in tears, but nothing I could say would dissuade him. He has convinced himself that my love is conditional and that God made him homosexual, so he has no choice.

My son walked out of my life that day without even a hug. I have not heard from him since. I have tried to make contact a couple of times but with no response.

So this is where things are now. I pray daily for his life to be touched in some way that will bring him back to where he belongs. I pray that he will have a right relationship with God and come out of a very deceptive and dangerous lifestyle.

* * * *

Kim: A Woman Finds Freedom from Same-Sex Attraction

As a young girl, I experienced quite a bit of neglect from my mother, as well as sexual abuse from my alcoholic father. I remember that as a little girl, I believed that I was supposed to be a boy but somehow had been given the wrong body parts. I mimicked boy behaviors and was considered a tomboy.

I desperately wanted my mother's affection and attention. Because I wasn't able to get that, I developed a strong survivor mentality. I believed that I needed to take care of myself because no one else would. I erected high walls of protection. As I entered high school, I sought the affections of my friends—not sexually, but more emotionally, and in a nurturing way. I felt very strange and guilty and confused about that. I was quite promiscuous, though I always stopped short of actually having intercourse (thanks to my Catholic upbringing). I craved physical touch from anyone.

When I entered college, I met a girl who was a year older than me. She was a Christian and very outwardly loving. I was attracted to her and to the love she had to give. I realized that I was lacking in something she had and asked her about that. She shared the gospel with me, and I made an initial commitment to God but without really understanding what I was doing. I had no knowledge of repentance or of changing my lifestyle. I just knew that I wanted what my friend had. She and I developed a close relationship, and she, being very physically loving, was someone I wanted to be with all the time. I found myself craving her hugs and her affirmation. Our relationship was never sexual, though there was an unspoken tension.

Two years later, still in college, I totally gave my life to God and received some measure of healing from Him. The deep craving for affection and nurturing from women lessened. But as I walked into adulthood and marriage, I realized there was a part of me that was not at all satisfied. Also, I began to allow my mind to wander into the territory of homosexual thoughts and daydreams. Many years later, when I married, I realized that I had a cavernous need within me for female nurturing and affection. At one point, I thought about leaving my husband and children to pursue a relationship like that. When I actually considered giving up my life as I knew it, I started crying out to God, telling Him that I could not go on living like this. I told Him that either He had to meet that need in me or I would have to leave Him and try to get it met by the only way I thought it could be met—in a relationship with a woman. I had never felt anything so deeply as I felt that need.

As I continued to cry out to God and read His word, I came across the story of the woman at the well, recorded in John 4. When Jesus said to that woman that if she drank the well water she would thirst again; but if she drank of the water He would give her, it would become in her a spring of living water (see v. 13), finally I saw a ray of hope. I clung to that passage, and God showed me two things: (1) that she had to drink of the well water to live. Translation: It's not wrong to satisfy a felt need (in God-approved ways of course); and (2) that if I only satisfied my felt need, I would continue to become thirsty; in fact, my thirst would be ever increasing, because there is a deeper need that only God can fill by His Holy Spirit. And when He meets that need, the Spirit actually becomes a spring of living water in me.

I claimed that passage for myself and began to ask God to be true to His Word and satisfy my deep loss and need for the love of a mother. At the same time, I shared about my struggle with a couple of trusted friends and allowed them to meet my felt need in appropriate ways and to hold me accountable. I can't tell you exactly how it happened, but God met that need in me and began to quench my thirst in a way I didn't know was possible. He gave to me the love of a mother that I had never experienced and took away my desire to receive that love from another woman.

At that point, I became willing to renew my mind and not allow my thoughts to run free with homosexual thoughts. This was hard work, but it was totally do-able, because my thirst was being satisfied.

I guess the one thing I want to communicate to the homosexual is that his or her needs are real and they demand to be met. But if God isn't allowed to meet those needs in the depths of the person's soul, then he or she will always thirst and never be satisfied. In fact, it is my experience—and as I have talked with homosexuals, it seems to be their experience too—that the need only gets greater when you try to feed it with ungodly solutions (with a same-sex relationship). My passion is for someone who is living homosexually to discover God's character and experience His healing as He meets their deepest inner needs.

* * * *

Jane: Finding Strength and Comfort in Spite of the Pain

After many years of marriage, many years of struggle, many years of pain, I had come to acknowledge that my marriage was dead. The pain of realizing that my hopes and dreams wouldn't come to pass is something I'm still working through.

I've taken a lot of comfort in the words of Isaiah 43. God says, "When you pass through the waters, I will be with you; and when you pass through the rivers, they will not sweep over you. When you walk through the fire, you will not be burned; the flames will not set you ablaze" (v. 2).

Notice that He didn't say *if* I pass through the waters, but rather, *when* I pass through the waters. I never wanted the deep struggles of life to touch my family. But they did. I knew of my husband's struggles around homosexuality from the beginning, but I didn't have much understanding with that knowledge, because I didn't understand the roots, the deep pain and the difficulty in overcoming those issues.

I thought the struggles were finished when we married. But for many reasons, the marriage was difficult from the start. After a number of years, I found out that my husband had experienced repeated falls.

This devastated me.

I took the blame, telling myself that if I had been a better wife, if I had prayed more, and so on, this wouldn't have happened. At the same time, I kept the issue to myself. Although God didn't want me to bear it alone, I did. I didn't want to deal with the judgment that would likely come from the church.

As I have opened up a little, I find that I am not alone. Now I am holding on to God's promise that He has a plan for me, for my future, for hope (see Jer. 29:11). God is faithful. He is meeting all my needs. Even through the waters, the river, and the fire, God has been with me. They have not swept over me nor set me ablaze.

*   *   *   *

Lauren: A Daughter's Love for Her Gay Father

I believe my story is truly one that warrants the title of "preciously bittersweet." It would literally take hours to explain to you what has occurred in my life over the years—all the pain, fear, happiness, tears, joy, misery and even sometimes, shame. But to make it simple, I think only two statements are completely necessary: (1) I love my daddy with everything in me, and (2) I have found undeserved and amazing love in a heavenly Father that fills up everything and fixes all the hurt that has ever wounded me in my past or that will surely wound me in my future.

My parents divorced when I was a freshman in high school. After attempting to swallow the horrible discomfort that came from my mom's shocking words, "Your daddy and I are getting divorced," the bigger blow followed. "Daddy is gay." Those three words changed the course of my life forever; but God has made good of it!

One can imagine the pain that a young girl in high school would experience realizing that the image she had painted of her father was totally destroyed. One can imagine how hard it must be to explain to every important person in your life that your father is gay, and all the other "stuff" that goes with it. One can imagine the sadness and the tears of preparing for the wedding that will bring together two lovers of Christ, and in the midst of that, remembering all of the brokenness within her own parents' marriage.

But truly, the biggest struggle has come during the past four years, as my life and my walk with Christ have grown deeper. I have known Jesus since I was very young, but in these past few years, God has walked through the open door of my heart, which I admit had been shut at times; and He has come in with huge thunder and with generous open arms. I now realize how loved I am by my heavenly Father, and how, even in the midst of my own transgressions and wrong choices, the Lord still calls on me and calls me His own. I believe and depend on the fact that He desires to know me; and I know that I am His child and fully loved.

I love my daddy. I have seen him become hugely successful at his career. I have seen him love and respect his family and friends. I see the potential he has, the kind heart that yearns to be present more often, and the light of the Lord that shines in him as surely as it brightens me. Unfortunately, I have also been witness to the extremely sad, lonely and very selfish life that has completely engulfed him as he has fallen prey to the Enemy and has embraced the homosexual lifestyle.

The more that Daddy has opened up to being gay, the less kind and loving he is, and the more selfish he has become. As a daughter who cares for her father and loves him unconditionally, that is extremely difficult for me to admit. I think it's very important for me to know that his being gay *is his* choice. We are all made in the beautiful likeness of God our Creator, and all I can say to those who would argue differently is that Satan is very tricky and he doesn't think twice about haunting sweet children and having them believe the father of lies. I am aware of how real the Enemy is in our everyday life. I know that I am not completely free from his cunningness. It is in recognizing this that I have realized how my father's sins are no different from my own. God doesn't see one sin as greater or lesser than another; He only calls us to repent and be forgiven and to go forward with His name embedded on our chests.

Sadly, I have not yet seen any signs of my daddy wanting to shed this part of his life. Our culture has made it extremely easy and acceptable for people to be gay; it is almost welcomed. This makes me tearful because I know the Truth and I refuse to water down the gospel and make it fit my father's life choices, or even fit my own; and believe me, that is hard, and there have been plenty of times when I would love to do just that. I also have seen firsthand what pain comes with his choosing the homosexual lifestyle. There is pain for everyone involved; and my daddy, though he may say he is "happy" and has "found himself," is truly not.

I said that my story is bittersweet, because even in the midst of all of my trials and tribulations, now at age 25, I can see how God has brought me closer to Him and has made me depend on Him. I am constantly brought back to the fact that the Lord knows me specifically, and He knows what I can and can't handle. Even though sometimes I want to scream "I can't take anymore! I really think this should be it!" I love the Lord, and I know that my pain has been a huge part of this unfolding love story.

When I want Daddy to be a father so desperately; when I want to not hear him talk about his boyfriend; when I hide myself in my future husband's arms, weeping over the idea of someday explaining all of this to our children and possibly making restrictions on how they can spend time with their grandfather; when I want, at times, to not even spend time with him because I know I'm going to hear or see things that make me uncomfortable, sad, and angry; when I can barely stand the feeling I get when I think of how my precious brother must be desiring so badly to have a godly man in his life and to have that man be his father, then I am reminded of Christ's love for me and how I am called to love my father in the same way. I am reminded of the death of Christ on the cross and how it should have been my blood instead of His.

Remembering these things doesn't make it easier, but it reminds me that I am under persecution here on Earth and that my promise of eternity with the Father will wash away all of the bad. Until that time comes, every day I pray for Daddy. I pray that I could just continue to love him in spite of the hurtful things he does to me and to himself; and I pray that one day he will know the freedom that comes from giving everything over to the Lord, and finally say, "I admit that I can't do anything without You; I am in desperate need of something more, and I know that You are it." This is the Daddy I have been waiting for!

*　　*　　*　　*

Elizabeth: Her Husband Lives Homosexually
After 30 Years of Marriage

Everyone goes through difficult periods in life. The challenge is how to get through them—not just to survive them, but to thrive in the midst of them.

I had some major health problems several years ago. It was a very hard time for me and my family. I had a lot of time to think while I was in the hospital—to wonder, why me? Yet I did live through that difficult time of waiting and surgery.

And so I thought that being given a second chance at life also meant that my trials were over.

Not really.

Two years ago, I had additional surgery. Complications set in and I almost died. The doctors also found cancer in one of my kidneys. After several days in the ICU, and a very long recovery, I began to think I was going to make it again. Were my trials over this time?

Not at all. During the past several years, my marriage had been dying a slow, agonizing death. I kept thinking that things would improve, but they didn't. Last year, on the week of my birthday, my husband came out of the closet and moved out.

I could never have dreamed that this would happen to me, to us, or that I would be living alone at this time in my life, with this betrayal and pain. Those things happened to other people, not to me. Not to my family. We were the perfect family, with the perfect children. We were supposed to live happily ever after. How were we going to get through this? How do we go on with our lives when everything we've known for so many years is taken away? I can truly say that I couldn't have survived without the Lord taking my hand and leading me through the dark days.

At first, it was hard for me to go to sleep at night. My mind would work overtime on all of the problems. I can't tell you how many times I prayed for the Lord to wrap His arms around me, comfort me and put me to sleep. And He did. He gave me the strength to keep going.

We all know deep down that no one has the perfect family. We don't live in a fairy tale world. We don't always live happily ever after. God didn't promise that. He did promise to be there for us during the dark days. When we are living in difficult days, the question is, How do we keep going?

Let me tell you about some things I have learned that have helped me.

I learned that I can have a new dream for my life. My dream for my family had to change. I had always seen my husband and me enjoying our children and grandchildren together for the rest of our lives. That dream had to have a new chapter. Changing the way I viewed the rest of my life was very difficult, but it wasn't impossible. Slowly, I have been able to see my life without him and to be okay with that.

I learned to be more thankful for my children. I have always loved and supported my children; but to see them as caring, responsible adults is an added blessing. All three of my children have grown into wonderful people who I am very proud of. They have been so supportive of me since the separation. In the first few weeks, they called me every day, sometimes twice a day. It wasn't easy to see my children hurt; and they have been hurt and are still hurting. But together, we are growing stronger and are working through our feelings.

I learned that I can make my own decisions. I had to buy a car soon after my husband left. My car was on its very last "leg." I thought, *What do I know about buying a car? I've never done that alone.* It felt so wonderful when I signed the papers on my car. I felt very grown up. I thought, *If I can do this, I can make it.*

I had married in my twenties and had never lived alone. I wondered how I would survive the loneliness. Although I'm not afraid to be alone, being alone after years of having someone else in the house took some getting used to. I am so thankful for family and friends who have been there for me when I'm hurting.

I learned that I don't have to be angry about my situation. I'm not going to tell you that I didn't feel angry or resentful, but I did *not* let it take over my life. It did no good to harbor ill feelings—that only made me ill! And spending all my time and energy being angry didn't help. It drained me emotionally and spiritually. I had to let the Lord take care of the person who had hurt me.

I have learned to live each day and be thankful for it. I decided to make the most of every day and not take the time I had with my family for granted.

Several months before the separation, I decided that my greatest desire was to get through this separation with as much grace and dignity as possible. Most days, I have succeeded.

My hope is that if anyone reading this is experiencing a difficult time right now, he or she will find encouragement to keep moving forward.

*   *   *   *

Saralee: A Mother and Her Son Reestablish Their Relationship

B.—my first child—was born in January 1986. I wrapped my world around him; I used him to help fulfill my life and make up for the fact that I had an empty marriage. His father (whom I will call T.) spent very little time with him; T. was always working or playing golf.

B. grew up to be what most would call a momma's boy. When he was around six years old, T. and I divorced.

T. was a very unemotional man. I was told that he had not been reared in an affectionate family. When I was eight months' pregnant with B., I found a letter from T's ex-wife in his truck. The letter told him that they couldn't get back together and that he needed to make his mind up to stay with me and make a life. Needless to say, I was crushed. There I was, pregnant with his child, and he was busy entertaining his ex-wife. I guess that explained why he couldn't show me any love; he was too busy still showing it to his ex. I took the letter to him and asked if he wanted to explain it to me. He just looked at me and said he had nothing to say.

After seven years of begging T. for affection and finding myself looking elsewhere for it, we decided to divorce.

Our son became very close to me and to my mother. I guess we were what you would call his heroes. If only I had known the importance of a relationship between a son and father, I might not have lived with the sadness of that loss.

When our son began school, it was hard for him—overwhelming, in fact—to detach from my mother and me. Most days he went to school crying. Of course the other kids made fun of him. Kids can be very cruel. They began to call him names. "Fag" was at the top of the list.

When he started second grade, I married a man who had two older boys from a previous marriage. We tried to put the two families together. Unfortunately, this man looked at my son the same way as his schoolmates. I can remember that when B. was in the fifth grade, my husband told him he was going to be nothing but a "fag" when he grew up. After five years, this marriage ended. He went back to his ex-wife, and B. and his younger brother and I were once again on our own.

The years rocked on. There was never any true male role model for my sons. In 1997, I married again for all the wrong reasons. My new husband and I fought all the time. I had a little girl while married to him, but the marriage ended after he turned on my sons. I spent the next two-and-a-half years letting God heal my brokenness. I did not date anyone. I only devoted my life to God and to my kids. We went to church. For three years, B. was very active with the youth group. I was amazed that a young man could have such a strong relationship with God. B. hung around with the youth pastor a lot. Finally a male role model to look up to!

At the end of his junior year, he wanted to try out for the cheerleading squad. When he approached me about it, all I thought was, *Haven't you had enough?* But his mind was made up. He proved to be outstanding as a cheerleader. His fellow classmates, even the ones who had been calling him names, voted him on the squad. Not only did he make cheerleader, but he also made prom king his senior year.

But that year, he also began to change and rebel. We began to fight. Everything I did and said was wrong. Suddenly, the son I thought I was so close to began pulling away. He began to talk about boys from other towns that I had no idea how he knew. He would say that he had met them in summer track or something like that. He began to fall away from all the youth-group activities at church. I saw a side of him that I didn't know existed. The fights continued, and he ended up moving in with my mother and finishing his senior year. He was tired of being the "good Christian boy." If I had only known all the pain he was feeling. All this time, while God was healing me and mending my brokenness, Satan was tearing my son apart.

I married a Christian man in 2004, the same year B. graduated. My relationship with B. was still strained. I will never forget the day I came right out and asked him if he was gay. My heart broke when he said yes.

From that day forward my mind was consumed with nothing else. I began to go over every little detail of his life. What did I do to cause this to happen? What could I have done to prevent this? I blamed myself for all of it. I remember walking down the gravel road leading to our house, crying my eyes out and talking and screaming to God. I began to remember all those times that I had fought for my son when someone had called him "fag" or "queer."

We tried to talk a few times, but it usually only ended in fights and swearing.

The months rolled on. I didn't hear from him much. When I would call him, either he wouldn't answer or he kept the conversation very short. This was so hard for me. Our relationship had changed from best friends to what seemed like enemies. If I had only known that he was dealing with so many emotions that he didn't even know how to express them.

All I could do was pray. And that's what I did. Once again, God was speaking to me through my pain and heartache. I spent many months on my knees. (It's so amazing how God meets you where you are.) I picked myself up and started working on what *I* could do to better understand my son. I started reading. The first book I read was *When Homosexuality Hits Home* by Joe Dallas. This book gave me a whole new view of where I fit into all of this. I had to go back and walk in B.'s shoes—feel the pain he felt for so many years, understand the scars he carries with him on a daily basis. I must say that the pain was unbearable.

After a time, I was ready to talk with him. I called him and we met for dinner. I prayed the whole time I was traveling to meet him that God would give me the words to say. When I sat down, I was just about to burst inside; then we started talking. I told him about the book I had read and that I had put myself in his shoes and had felt his pain. I told him that I was so sorry for causing any part of his pain. This was the beginning of a whole new relationship for us. Just hearing my acceptance of him opened the door. I told him that I didn't agree with what he was doing, but I felt more understanding about the fact that he was gay. I let him know that he had a family who loved him and wanted to see him. I told him that he had a little sister who thought he hung the moon, and she deserved to see her brother.

Since that talk, we have been able to have a better relationship. I know now that I can once more talk to him about anything. I know that more answers will come in time. I will not push. I will just pray—and never stop praying—that someday my son will see the light that I have seen.

*   *   *   *

Dinah: A Woman Finds That Her Perfect Marriage Was a Facade

When a divorced woman begins the conversation with the words, "We had a perfect marriage," I've come to anticipate that sooner or later she will reveal that her husband is gay. Dinah was so gentle and tender-hearted when she told me her story.

I said, "It sounds as if you still love him!"

"How could I not love him?" she replied. "I *still* love him."

I am appalled, my old bitterness seeping out. "How could you not be angry—even furious? He ruined your marriage." I can't believe her. How does she do it?

"I guess it's because I was so worried about his drastic changes. All I could think about was that he was going crazy—something very awful was happening to my husband. Until just two years prior, I thought we had a nearly *perfect marriage!* Our friends wished their marriages were like ours—we were best friends, we talked about everything. He was charming, a complete extrovert, wonderfully fun. He loved to go shopping with me. We did everything together. We helped couples with their marriage problems, even counseled friends who were struggling with homosexuality.

"But in the space of two years, all of that changed. He started being cool to me; he was not at home as much as usual; and then one day, he told me he wanted to be single. I didn't have a clue about what was going on. Then he confronted me with a list of rules, out of the blue.

1. Don't talk to me except for one hour after dinner.
2. Don't tell me how you feel.
3. Don't ask how I feel.
4. Don't touch me unless I say it's okay.

"When things started getting very strange, I asked him to go to counseling with me. He said he would go, but only one time. He would go on the condition that he could tell the therapist what was wrong with me and what I needed to do. It wasn't to be about him.

"When I went back the next week by myself, the counselor asked me about our sexual relationship. I knew she must be probing to see if I had thought of homosexuality. Then she said it. 'Have you considered the possibility that he is a homosexual?'

"I felt ashamed and guilty of my thoughts. What a terrible accusation. What if it weren't true and I hadn't waited to see if he were proven innocent. I was horrified to think that I would ever think such a thing. We had been married for 20 years. Surely this couldn't be true!

"What he said to me a year or so later was that he didn't regret our life together or consider them wasted years. He always wished that he could have been the man I wanted and needed. However, he was convinced that much of his secret pain, misery and anger stemmed from his denying who he really is and working so hard to suppress the reality of who he has always been. He said that he tried so hard to conform to the 'norm' and thought that much of the time he had succeeded.

"He told me that he chose at an early age to live his life according to the expectations of those he loved and admired, wishing to emulate what was 'normal.' What he really did, he said, was to sell himself out and throw himself into a deep dark hole. He said he spent three decades of his life unconsciously punishing himself for doing so.

"Some of his friends told him that he was living a decadent life now; but he says he is living the truth. He says that most Christians really don't want to face the truth or deal with it. He thinks that it wouldn't matter if he were living a completely celibate life; some would still consider him in need of being fixed as long as he considered himself as he is.

"He finally said that he was content and happy being who he is, even though the majority of society cannot or will not accept it. He said that he was thankful that God is more understanding, more loving and more comprehensively embracing than his fellow human beings. He ended by saying that out of all the concerns he had about his leaving, my welfare was his greatest concern."

*   *   *   *

Karen: A Mother Whose Son Is Gay

My story started when my second son went off to college. He lived on campus at a large university and would come home from time to time for home-cooked meals or to do laundry. We thought things were going well.

His sophomore year was a different story. He lived at home and commuted to college his first semester. In that time, we noticed that he spent a lot of time on his cell phone very late at night. He had a lot of friends—always did in high school, too. He went to every dance and to prom. We thought he was seeing somebody, but he was very vague about the person. He would bring home a buddy we thought he had met at school. We couldn't put our finger on it, but things were different. God began to reveal many small details that caused us to finally ask our son if he was gay. We wanted to be wrong; we prayed that we were wrong. But we were right.

The emotions we experienced totally overwhelmed us. This had not even been on our radar. We were a normal middle-class family. We were active members of a small conservative evangelical church that we had been members of since our children were very little. Why, our sons had attended Sunday School, VBS, Backyard Bible Clubs, youth events, mission trips—you name it. Most of our closest friends were members of our church, and we had a pretty close family network. Both sets of grandparents lived close by.

We were faced with our own personal dilemma. What if our friends found out? What would they say? We kept this a secret from everyone, including our family. It was too difficult to think about, let alone tell someone about it. They would certainly judge our parenting skills and be critical about things that could have been done better.

Finally, my sister asked in a very concerned and sincere tone, "What is going on?" I felt that God had been prodding me to say something to her. So I told her my story with deep sobs and anguish. She responded with tremendous compassion and concern for us, and for our son. After all, she loved her nephew very much. She had seen him grow up and spent time with him. My sister told me there was no way to prevent this, as we had no outward signs. She prayed about him daily and finally sent him an e-mail. At this point, our son had completely cut off contact with us because he didn't want to live under our roof any more. My husband struggled with what to say to him, because an argument seemd to always occur when they talked. My sister sent this e-mail to our son:

Dear _____

I realize seeing this e-mail is unexpected!

I got your e-mail address from your mom and have asked her some direct questions about what is going on. She has shared with me because we are close, and I care. Despite what choices you have made and are making in your life, and the path you have chosen right now, you need to be reminded that you are loved, no matter what. I am your "Auntie," spoken in that endearing way I have since you were born. Nothing will ever change that. Your uncle and I want you to know that our door is open, our phone is on and we would love to know where you are. We would love to talk to you if you ever want to talk.

What is going on does not change how we view you, or the fact that we love you. You are family, our nephew and irreplaceable.

We miss you and have missed you. In case you don't have our number handy, it is _____.

Love, Aunt _____

This e-mail sparked a very kind response by our son. He appreciated that his aunt loved him unconditionally, and he was glad his mom had someone to share this with.

I have looked for many resources from the Focus on the Family website and ran across the Love Won Out conference page. To my utter shock, one of the keynote speakers was a woman who worked in the same building as I did and had contact with my department. I wept. God had sent a life preserver to me. I immediately e-mailed her and received such wonderful, godly counsel. She also put me in contact with another woman who has a similar story to mine. This woman in turn connected me with another woman with a similar story. We have now met together and continue to lift each other up in prayer and encouragement. I truly consider these Christian gals to be my friends. We have a special bond—we know how each other feels and can relate to the pain and struggles that we all face.

My husband and I are having more contact with our son and will be supportive of him as best as we can. We never stop praying for him.

*   *   *   *

Stephanie: A Couple's Story

In the summer of 1996, after only two years of marriage, my husband announced that he didn't want to be married and was not attracted to me. Quite literally, I freaked out. He quickly recanted and blamed his discontentment on being depressed and unfulfilled at work. So he decided to go back to school and pursue another career.

On November 1, 1996, I came home from work to find a letter taped to the front door. I could never have imagined what I would read in that letter. Mike took several pages to tell me that he was gay and had always been gay, that he didn't love me, and that he wanted a divorce. My dream of living happily ever after was shattered.

I didn't know anything about homosexuality, but I trusted the promises of the Bible that the Lord can change anyone. I also knew that I had sought the Lord in regard to our relationship from our very first date, and that the Lord did not want our marriage to end in divorce. With the help of our parents and a few close friends, I began looking for a counselor, a book or a program to fix the situation and get Mike to change his mind. In spite of these efforts, Mike left and jumped completely into the gay lifestyle.

During the first months of our separation, I experienced emotions more intensely than ever before—anger, confusion, frustration, loneliness, fear. I looked for peace in every conversation, every book, every song. But the only times I found true comfort and peace were when I was reading my Bible and when I was on my face before the Lord in prayer.

Nothing I did seemed to be working to bring Mike home. Finally, I realized that I was worrying about Mike when the Lord wanted to change *me*. I realized that my life would never be the same—that I would either be divorced or I would be married to a man I really didn't know. If I was to survive, God would have to do a work in my own heart. I continued to pray for Mike, but this was a turning point for me, and I began to submit myself to the Lord for His work in me.

Around the same time, and without my knowledge, the Lord was beginning to work on Mike's heart. He began to see how the gay theology did not line up with Scripture. His grandmother, who knew none of the reasons behind our separation, sent him a note simply stating that she loved him and that he was always welcome in her home. Mike wondered for the first time if someone could truly love him unconditionally.

At an intense time of conflict between Mike and me, and during the same week that he had determined to file the divorce papers, his dad gave him the book *You Don't Have to Be Gay* by Jeff Konrad. It was the first testimony Mike had heard of someone finding freedom from homosexuality. Mike wrestled with the Lord about coming back home and all the trials that were sure to come. The response the Lord gave him was "I love you." Mike realized that the love of the Lord was more than sentimental; it was powerful. And he realized that the Lord would walk with him through whatever trials lay ahead.

One evening in April 1997, Mike came to our house and offered to mow the lawn for me. That evening he came inside and asked to come back home. He couldn't make any promises about physical intimacy or whether or not he would want to have children, but he was willing to recommit to our marriage. I was shocked. I had a choice, and out of obedience to the Lord, I chose to recommit myself to the marriage. We stood in the kitchen at opposite corners of the room and stared at each other. We were both hurt and wounded. We had no loving feelings for each other and we didn't even know where to start; but we both believed that the Lord would honor our commitment.

The next couple of years were very hard. We moved back to the town where we had lived 10 months before. We had a few close friends there who knew the details of our marital struggles. And we joined a Bible-teaching church. We also had a godly counselor who poured into Mike what it means to be a man in Christ. We worked through the struggles of giving and receiving forgiveness; we learned how to communicate, rebuild trust and make our marriage and home a safe place. People often ask me how I was able to forgive Mike. It was simply obedience to God. After experiencing brokenness and the Lord's forgiveness over sins I had committed in college, the Lord gave me a willing heart to forgive Mike. However, while I forgave him quickly, it took considerable time for the trust in our marriage to be restored.

Soon after Mike moved back home, and after we had a fight one evening, we read 1 Peter 5:6: "Humble yourselves, therefore, under God's

mighty hand, that he may lift you up in due time." We humbled ourselves before the Lord and He truly has lifted us up. He has given us a
love for one another beyond our understanding, and certainly beyond
anything we could have imagined. He has restored trust and intimacy
between us. He has blessed us with three beautiful children. And He has
given us opportunities to minister to others—to comfort others with the
comfort we have received. He has shown Himself to us as powerful and
gracious and loving—keeping all of His promises.

* * * *

Tarese: A Mother Whose Son Lives Homosexually

After four years of marriage, our only child, S., was born. He was a very good child, and easy to raise. He regularly attended church and Sunday School, and at the age of nine, he asked Jesus to come into his life and was baptized. He continued to attend church through high school.

In school, S. was put in accelerated classes and did well in academics. Outside of school, he was more interested in artistic things rather than sports. Around ninth or tenth grade, he seemed to go through a very dark period. His bedroom showed expressions of his inner feelings—dead flowers hanging around, outrageous pictures of musical groups, and so on. However, he was never involved with drugs or alcohol, so we thought this was just a phase. There were other things that happened about this time that I realize now I should have questioned. How naïve parents can be!

In high school, he dressed in black most of the time and did some crazy things with his hair. He had girlfriends as well as guy friends and would attend dance clubs with his friends. I believe this was the time when he started questioning his sexuality. After high school, he moved out to share an apartment with a friend and began attending cosmetology school.

Because of employment, we moved away but returned for a visit a couple years later. After being confronted by his father, S. finally told us the truth (after lying to us for years) about living a homosexual lifestyle. (His dad was facing reality while I was probably in denial.) After talking with S. for some time, we returned home, where all the emotions came pouring out—anger, rage, hurt, sadness, depression, loss, endless crying. We thought often about the hopes and dreams we had for our only child, which we would never experience—a wedding, a wife to share his life, grandchildren to love and cherish.

We asked him to come and live with us for a year and get some counseling to help him understand all the things going on in his life and help him make some different choices. He refused to do this. The relationship was so difficult for many years. Finally, our mother/son relationship began to heal; but the father/son relationship was almost nonexistent during this time. This relationship slowly began to change for the better;

but only a short time went by before my husband passed away.

Slowly but steadily my relationship with my son is improving. My deep love for him will never cease. Though the tears continue, with God's constant and abiding love, we will make it.

One of the things I'm working on is how to listen—how to really hear and understand what my son is saying (and feeling) without my trying to come up with an answer. I have been learning to present my beliefs and tell him what's on my heart, not in an argumentative way but in a calm, loving and rational way. He disagrees with many things I say, and I have learned to just accept where he's coming from at that particular time, even when I disagree.

S. is able to talk quite openly with me. He seems to be different with me when he's away from his partner—he's more willing to share his feelings. He still has a rebuttal for many things we discuss; but when he doesn't, he appears to consider what I share with him. He's willing to read short articles about things that are too complicated for me to explain.

One important thing on my part is to know when enough is enough. I have to know when we need to move on to other subjects and just have fun together, which we do. Because he's my only child, we have shared a lot together, and I think we both enjoy being with each other. I have to remember there are so many other things to share with him without having to discuss the issue of homosexuality during every visit or phone conversation. I now realize that I'm not going to change S.; only God, in His way and in His time, can do that. I trust in the verse that says God will give me the desires of my heart when I diligently seek Him (see Ps. 37:4).

My prayer is that God will intervene in S's life—that the Holy Spirit will open his heart and mind to see and embrace the truth and bring him back into a right relationship with Jesus, which he entered into when he was nine years old.

And my prayer is for God to work in my life to love my son unconditionally and accept him just as he is, while I don't approve of his lifestyle. God is faithful, and my hope is in Him!

*   *   *   *

Endnotes

Chapter 1
1. John 11:4

Chapter 3
1. Matthew 24:43
2. Judges 13:7

Chapter 4
1. Jeremiah 29:11

Chapter 6
1. Isaiah 63:9

Chapter 7
1. Exodus 23:20-23,24
2. 1 Thessalonians 5:18
3. Esther 4:14
4. See Luke 12:48
5. See Luke 7:47
6. Hosea 1:10; Romans 9:25-26
7. Matthew 9:37; Luke 10:2

Chapter 8
1. Luke 15:11-24
2. Darlene Zschech, "The Potter's Hand," © 1997, Hillsongs Australia.
3. Bruxy Cavey, "Responding to the Gay Marriage Debate," Version 1.2, Spring 2005, from a newsletter for his church.

Chapter 9
1. 2 Corinthians 5:19
2. Ezekiel 22:30
3. Psalm 106:23
4. Matthew 28:19
5. Hebrews 13:2
6. Bruxy Cavey, "Responding to the Gay Marriage Debate," Version 1.2, Spring 2005.
7. John Leland, "New Cultural Approach for Conservative Christians," the *New York Times*, Arts section, December 26, 2005.
8. Ibid.

Chapter 10
1. 1 Corinthians 2:9-10, emphasis added.
2. John 17: 25-26, emphasis added.
3. See 1 Corinthians 10:13
4. See James 1:2-4
5. See Judges 6:12,13
6. James 5:16
7. Isaiah 40:27-31

8. Romans 4: 16,18,19, 20-23, 24
9. Philippians 3:10
10. Leif Enger, *Peace Like a River* (New York: Grove Press, 2001), n.p.
11. Bruce Wilkinson, Secrets of the Vine (Sisters, OR: Multnomah Publishers, Inc.), n.p.
12. Ibid., n.p.
13. Ephesians 1:17-20
14. George MacDonald, *At the Back of the North Wind* (New York: David McKay, Publisher, 1919; William Morrow and Company), p.65.
15. Ephesians 3:20
16. Pablo Perez, "My God Is King," Forerunner Music, 2005.

Chapter 11

1. Exodus is a Christian interdenominational information and referral ministry addressing homosexual issues and ministering to ex-gays.
2. Esther 4:14
3. James 1:2, *Phillips*
4. Deuteronomy 8:2

Chapter 12

1. James 1:1, *Phillips*

WORDS OF HOPE
AND HEALING

**Release the Pain,
Embrace the Joy**
Help for the Hurting Heart
Michelle McKinney Hammond
ISBN 08307.37227

**I'm Pregnant...
Now What**
Heartfelt Advice on
Getting Through an
Unplanned Pregnancy
Ruth Graham and *Sara Dormon*
ISBN 08307.35755

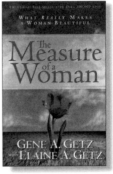

**The Measure
of a Woman**
What Really Makes a
Woman Beautiful
Gene A. Getz with
Elaine A. Getz
ISBN 08307.32861

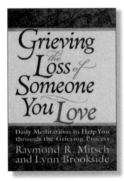

**Grieving the Loss of
Someone You Love**
Daily Meditations to Help
You Through the
Grieving Process
Raymond Mitsch and
Lynn Brookside
ISBN 08307.34368

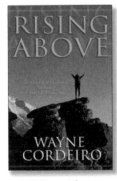

Rising Above
Living a Life of Excellence
No Matter What Life
Throws at You
Wayne Cordeiro
ISBN 08307.36328

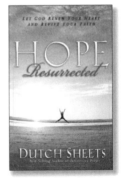

Hope Resurrected
Let God Renew Your Heart
and Revive Your Faith
Dutch Sheets
ISBN 08307.36247